Luxembourg

The grand duchy and its people

George Renwick

Alpha Editions

This edition published in 2019

ISBN : 9789353891183

Design and Setting By
Alpha Editions
email - alphaedis@gmail.com

LUXEMBOURG:

THE GRAND DUCHY
AND ITS PEOPLE

BY

GEORGE RENWICK, F.R.G.S.

AUTHOR OF

"ROMANTIC CORSICA" AND "FINLAND TO-DAY"

WITH 34 ILLUSTRATIONS AND A MAP

NEW YORK

CHARLES SCRIBNER'S SONS

597-599 FIFTH AVENUE

E V.

A.292527

TO

MARGARET

CONTENTS

ILLUSTRATIONS

A RURITANIA OF TO-DAY

Denn das ist, bei meiner Ehre,
Doch ein allerliebster Ort.

GOETHE.

CHAPTER I

A RURITANIA OF TO-DAY

THE world appears to be fast outgrowing its Ruritanias. We are in an era of vast states and huge empires ; there is not a little land but is threatened, more or less alarmingly, by a powerful neighbour, ready to throw out a bayonet-bristling frontier and so add yet more to the fabric of wide dominion. What Ruritanias have gone to make our empires of to-day, and with their going what romance has ended ! What individuality and personality have often been swallowed up by the Moloch of Might, crushed in the arms of Ambition !

But it is not only the imperial desire for the biggest possible " place in the sun " which is robbing the world of its Ruritanias. The Empire of Speed is one of the greediest. Its people think little of wrecking an Arcadia ; they slaughter Beauty on their dusty altar without a thought :

> Motors take the road !
> (Take the *whole* of the road ;)
> Snort and quiver in dreadful play !
> (Earthquakes out for a holiday),

Burn the miles of the winding way !
Shriek to the cloudlands o'er us. . . .
Like the swoop and rush of a runaway star
Is the meteor flight of a motor-car !

And, to be quite just, it does not need the possession of a motor-car to make the tourist a tyrant. Oh, how many lands delectable he has spoiled with char-à-banc and belvedere ! How many delightful, kindly folks he has infected with the germ of commercialism and artificiality ! And that Alexander is ever looking out for new worlds to conquer. Yet I connive at his conquests ! If, however, he accepts me as co-conspirator, let me plead with him that he learn something of the art of travel. It is better to know a county than to rush, in stress and strain, across a continent. Be a wanderer.

So let me say this : It is fatal to follow a guidebook, absurd to map out a route. Obtain from guides and maps, by all means, "the lie of the land," but leave them behind. If you do not often feel, with Stewart Edward White, that " the mere name of a place seems to strike deepest at the heart of romance," if you can feel and can resist the call of a name ten miles from the way a road may happen to be leading you, you are not a wanderer. If a chance word from a passing wayfarer will not make you turn aside and stake your chance of a bed and a supper, well, keep your gospel of speed and " travel in comfort." If your curiosity demands a certain accurately timed amount of satisfaction per day with regular hours for meals, by all means see that you have a circular ticket for a conducted tour.

Not to such do I offer my picture of an Arcadian duchy. This tiny paradise, this little unspoiled corner of earth which has known Nature's most happy inspirations, is for those whose guide is Wanderlust, for those who count the loss of speed and "all modern conveniences" "not too great a price to pay for the sight of a place called the Hills of Silence, for acquaintance with the people who dwell there, perhaps for a glimpse of the Saga-spirit that so named its environment." And, for reward, I promise them that they will return "laden with strange and glittering memories," if only they will follow, not necessarily in my footsteps, but wherever in its towns and villages, its softly undulating woods and stream-embroidered meadowlands, the little gods of the open air of this delectable Duchy may chance to call and to entreat.

The Grand Duchy of Luxembourg, a country a few square miles smaller than Cheshire, with the population of Edinburgh, lies hidden away in a corner between Belgium, France and Germany. If it is one of the smallest of European countries, it is one of the most beautiful. On the way to Switzerland and Italy, it is scarcely known to the European traveller ; the seeker after natural beauties has long regarded it as the Cinderella of the three Ardenne sisters. But well may the other two be jealous of the dowry Mother Nature gave to the little Duchy. Neither the Belgian nor the French Ardennes have such a rich and lovely succession of mount and valley, of forest and bush, of plain and gorge and river. No other little land provides such continual and varying delight for the wanderer. There Nature's great tome is condensed to a pocket volume ; there are her " selected works." How her caprice changes at every turn ! How her art charms with its infinite variety !

Not alone, coquette-like, on its beauty does the Duchy rely to cast a spell of attraction over those who would know her, for what is Luxembourg

> But that blessed brief
> Of what is gallantest and best
> In all the full-shelved Libraries of Romance ?

Over it are scattered relics which are the implements to help us lift Time's lava and trace a stirring story of a long-dead past. We find in it something of every ruler of Rome ; we can conjure up the Druids' grove. Cæsar with his legions takes us through the Forest of Arduenna. Huns ravaged it from end to end ; Attila left his name there. It was of the Empires of Charlemagne and Charles V. It gave five Emperors to Germany ; on its outskirts the house of Hohenzollern first took root. It bore the brunt of the Thirty Years War. It produced William the Silent, builder of the Dutch Republic. It has " right to pride," for it long held the centre of the stage in the great drama of European history.

To-day, the storms long over, it makes but little history, and is happy. Among the great nations of Europe it is a little Ruritania ; it might be the child of some novelist's imagination, a curious experiment in nation-making. It has a charming young Queen all its own—the Grand Duchess Marie Louise Adelheid ; it is independent and autonomous. The Duchy's army consists of just three hundred men with half a dozen officers. (It is rather unromantic, but still it must be said that the majority of those soldiers are generally employed in duties of a civil nature—as postmen, railwaymen, and customs officials.) Every male citizen whose taxes amount to twelve shillings or over per annum is entitled to a vote. The monarchy is constitutional ; the Grand Duchess nominates the Upper House of fifteen members, and there is a Chamber of forty-eight deputies, elected for six years, half of its number being returned every three years. In matters of government the Grand Duchess is assisted by a Conseil de Gouvernement, a sort of Cabinet, nominated by the monarch, and composed of four members. One is the President of the Upper House, the Conseil d'État, and three are called " directeurs généraux." The four share among them the different public departments, and are responsible to Parliament for their policy.

Curiously enough, there is no trial by jury. The country is divided into thirteen cantons—there has been no petition that the thirteenth should be numbered 12A or that the thirteen should be reduced to twelve or increased to fourteen !—and each has its justice de paix. A tribunal d'arrondissement sits at Luxembourg and another at Diekirch, and at the capital there is the High Court of Justice, which is the court of appeal and of cassation. The parliamentary voting list does duty for the election of the

2

local councils ; the Government selects the burgo-
masters, and not infrequently appoints some one outside the ranks of the elected.

Education is very highly developed in the Grand
Duchy, and many of the schools draw pupils from
far beyond the country's borders. There are nearly
eight hundred primary schools, in which education
is compulsory. Then come about seven hundred
" adult schools," and above them are the excellent
High Schools at Luxembourg, Diekirch and Echternach, the first named having well-organized industrial
and commercial sections. At Esch-on-Alzette is an
industrial institute, in which pupils are trained for
entry into all spheres in the world of business.
Ettelbrück has a large agricultural school, and in
the capital is one for the training of teachers and
another for artisans. The latter, which I saw at
work, is attended by over four hundred adults, all
eager to seize opportunities for education which were
not available when they were young. All those
schools are under State control, and it must be
admitted that for a population of little over a quarter
of a million very excellent educational provision is
thus made.

Considering its size, Luxembourg is an extraordinarily wealthy country. Agriculture is, of
course, the most important industry. Wheat, flax,
hemp and rape-seed are grown in large quantities ;
in a good season 1,250,000 gallons of wine will
be produced. Leather, gloves, pottery, cloth, paper,
beer and spirits and tobacco are mostly made in
such quantities as to permit of a brisk export trade.

Especially is this the case with regard to gloves.
Cattle, too, are reared in large numbers. Next to
agriculture, the greatest industry is the extraction
and smelting of iron ore. The canton of Esch is
blackened and blurred by furnaces, forges and
foundries, and the Grand Duchy produces no less
than one-fortieth of the world's supply of iron—a
tremendously high proportion. German enterprise
has not been blind to the industrial importance of
the Grand Duchy. Luxembourg is included in the
German Customs Union, and the direction of the
iron mines has come into the hands of a powerful
German combine.

Any real or apparent growth in the Germanization
of the Grand Duchy is looked upon with great dis-
favour and not a little dismay by the people. There
is no one a Luxembourger hates quite so much as
a Prussian, and the German control of the mines,
which meant the bringing of many German labourers
into the country, was at first regarded as the thin end
of the wedge. But the Duchy has recovered her
peace of mind ; the imported workers are not a
serious factor in Germanization. However happy
the Fatherland, the German emigrant has a curious
faculty for dismissing it quickly from mind and
affection. Unlike the Briton, he does not carry his
national manners and customs and interests with him.
He allows a new land to absorb him quickly. Many
Italian labourers have also been introduced, but it
has been found that both Italians and Germans
quickly internationalize themselves and exert no
foreign influence in the country. But if his

missionaries are bad, the German plods on slowly and, he hopes, surely. Luxembourg is in the German Zollverein ; her railway system is under German administration ; and at times persistent efforts are made to push German forward as the one official language of the country. The Duchy is, of course, bilingual. The Constitution of 1848 recognized the equality of both languages, though French has an advantage in being the official, parliamentary, administrative and judicial language, and so it holds its own fairly easily. In the primary schools instruction is given equally in French and German from the second year of study onward, but later the favour which French enjoys in administrative circles causes it to be almost exclusively used in instruction. German, however, counterbalances some of those advantages by the fact that it is a good deal easier for the people ; the working classes use it almost exclusively, and I found that officials were compelled to have recourse to it when dealing with rural and working people.

Then the Luxembourgers have their own peculiar patois, in which

> There wander, vague and clear,
> Strange vowels, mysterious gutturals.

And what a mixture that patois is ! Just as the country itself carries traces of all the peoples who have swept across it and dwelt in it, so the people's language has borrowed from at least a dozen tongues —from Celtic, Roman, Saxon, French and German, with others in between. It is not a written language in the full sense of the term. Over the thousand square miles of the Duchy it breaks itself up into at least four varieties. So any person who does write it can always plead "variety" if his spelling at Echternach is ridiculed at Wiltz. It is a case of spell as you please and as nearly phonetically as possible. Broadly, with a warp of Middle German a curiously mixed woof has produced a most fantastic texture. Saxon of the Conqueror's time and English words as they are to-day, French words with a distinct Dutch look, German nouns with their genders mixed—all help to make the disarray. Every race that has known Luxembourg either slightly or well has added an ingredient to the mixture ; inflections have gone, and simplicity reigns supreme. Spoken, the patois sounds like curious Dutch and bad German coming from a worn gramophone. In 1896 a proposal was put forward to admit the use of the patois in Parliament, but was set aside as unconstitutional.

To the archæologist and the geologist the Grand Duchy is extremely interesting. Celtic and Roman remains, altars built at the dawn of history, sepulchres of many races, magnificent mosaics and Roman roads, are still, in a large number of cases, well preserved. The geologist will find a very great deal that is interesting in this little land. The northern part, which is traversed by the Ardenne uplands, is called Osling. "A hundred pinnacles of grey and red-rust crags," rough masses of "old red sandstone," cut the landscape into quaintest pictures ; high plateaux covered with heath, wild ravines like deep wounds, wooded heights, valleys graceful and often rich in verdure, give Osling a peculiar beauty and distinguish it from that of the south, while into its slight severity Flora here and there throws her striking colours like tropic pearls cast on a sombre setting.

The name Osling, Oesling, or, as sometimes given, Eisling, has suggested to some the meaning of Ice Land, on account of the somewhat rigorous climate of the north of the Duchy as compared with the southern part. That, however, can scarcely be accepted. A reliable authority states : " The term Oesling has apparently come to us from the people who reached this country from the North. The first syllable, sounded variously as os, oes and ês, expresses the idea of ' link ' (chaînon) or ' brow ' (croupe) of hills. The Luxembourg dialect still retains the same syllable in Schellerois, which means ' shoulder ' or ' lesser chain ' (épaulement ou contrefort). Os (âs) is frequently found in the geographical terminology of Sweden to express the same idea as Joch, Rücken, Strang, as in Stifser Joch, Hunsrück and Haarstrang.

" With regard to the second syllable, ' ling,' it belongs to the old Norman language, in which lyng means heath (' lande ' or ' bruyère ' in French). In Swedish we have ' ljung,' in Danish ' lyng,' and in English ' ling ' has also been preserved as meaning heath or common heather (*Calluna vulgaris*). In Icelandic the form is the same as in English. The result, then, is to give a first meaning to Osling as the heath-covered brows of hills.

" But there is a second meaning, based on the translation of ' ling ' as brightness and light, and applied to snow-covered mountains. Then, Osling signifies the region of heath or of snow-covered mountains."

The same authority dismisses the spelling " Eisling " as absurd, because it leads to the meaning of land of heath or of oak (German : Eiche, oak), which is contrary to nature.

Luxembourg has, too, its own Switzerland, the glorious highlands of the east which garb themselves in all the colours of the sunlight. It is a pleasant change from the north to come upon the charming region, and yet again the south provides delightful variety for the lover of scenic beauty. There the geologist will see in successive gradations all the stages of the trias, lias and dogger formations, from streaked sandstone to polypier limestone. The southern district is called Gutland, and it is a country which well deserves its name. Hills of moderate height spread from end to end of it, a continuation of the sweeping undulations of loveliest Lorraine. Its plains are extremely fertile, the vegetation being in places luxuriant almost to a semi-tropical degree. The variety in the landscape here is infinite. The Mosel valley, for instance, is like a long wall of pictures by East ; yet not far away the Müllerthal presents, as it were, a challenging canvas of an Impressionist. All Creation's industry, indeed, and her most cunning chiselling have gone to give Luxembourg its radiant beauty and the continuous, changing surprise which it has. Sea, river,

rain, wind—all these, through the ages, have carved
the Grand Duchy's glories, and cut them magnificently.

Before we look more closely at the people of our
delectable Duchy and begin to wander through it,
let us see what storms of history they have passed
through. In religion, traditions, language, customs
and names we can trace the little nation's history
far back into the dull ages. Coins, weapons, trinkets,
domestic utensils are still found in her fields in considerable numbers, and they supply, letter by letter,
one of the most entrancing stories which Time has
to tell. The rough relics of the ancient Celtic priest
and beautiful examples of old Greek art are sometimes found lying together. Through Luxembourg,
then, the Gaul had returned from an invasion of
Greece and left belongings and booty behind. Wave
after wave of ancient peoples passed over the country,
each leaving its riddle on the sands to be read and
added to history. Luxembourg has borrowed from
all, but, true artist, has kept her individuality, has
yielded to every impress but has not lost her own
features. Old Gaul threw her frontiers round the
land which is Luxembourg to-day. Germanic peoples
and Celts mixed in and beside the country. By the
time that Julius Cæsar appears on the scene the
mingling of these races must have been far advanced,
for he describes the Trèvirians, dwellers from Mosel
to Meuse and Rhine, as half Gaul and half German,
that combination of chivalry and bravery stamped
deep on Europe to-day. The Roman, too, left his
mark, and of these three has come that race which

has stood so well one of the hardest and most fiery
of existences.

Schoolboys know well—or ought to—how the noble
Roman dealt with the Trèvirians, how he stiffened
his legions with them, how they helped to smash the
Nervii ; how Cæsar's Trèvirian enemy, Indutiomar,
was defeated, and how he perished in a river which
must have been one of Luxembourg's now peaceful
streams ; how the Trèvirians fought the cohorts of
Pompey, and were members of the Pretorian Guard
and among the finest soldiers of Rome. And in
Roman times, too, the Forest of Arduenna became
famous not only for its giant legionaries but for
its—fleshpots. How fatal was Luxembourg cookery,
famous still to-day, and praised by more than one
ancient writer, to that great Empire ! Was that
Ardenne art which has lived through the centuries—
and improved !—one of the factors which brought
about the wreck of Rome? At any rate, the Forest
of Arduenna provided much to heighten the revels of
decadent Rome.

Cæsar disappeared, but the Roman legions remained, covering the country with camps and cutting
it up with roads. Emperors oppressed the people
and stirred them to angry revolt. Tacitus takes
up the tale and unfolds the story of how Luxembourg
was devastated and soaked in blood for the first
time when the soldiers of Vespasian crushed the
rebellious Claudius Civilis. At Trèves the Emperors
of Rome held Court, and their presence spread a
certain amount of prosperity over a wide area, which
compensated for many generations for all the havoc

of war. But not for long. Soon the vespers of
Empire began to sound, and in the long-drawn-out
agony of Rome the country which we now call
Luxembourg suffered most terribly. Revolting
tribes swept in fiercest fury over it ; Huns brought
desolation. The Roman Empire fell, and the
Frankish Empire drew Luxembourg within it. Then
came the violent reign of the Merovingians, distinguished mainly for the war waged by the bloodthirsty Clovis, and in the smoke and ruin of the
conflagration he aroused the definite outline of
Luxembourg became faint and blurred. The Merovingians left no such traces as Celt and Roman, but
only scattered weapons and graves.

Charlemagne then created his Empire and left a
name. He brought into the Luxembourg country
thousands of Saxons who have left names on the
map and words, akin to English, in the language of
the people. With them came the Wiltzes, a tribe of
Pomerania, who gave Wiltz to Luxembourg and Wiltshire to England. And there was yet another link with
England. The Normans appeared with fire and sword
up Rhine and Mosel, penetrating as far as Remich.

Kings great and small, though mostly small, come
and go. Luxembourg has to submit to the most
bewildering changes in allegiance, country and
frontiers. Now it is part of High Lotharingia, then
of Low Lotharingia. But gradually, in the welter
of it all, the little country begins to stand out clearer
and clearer on the map and in the pages of history.
A descendant of Charlemagne, with the title of Count
of Ardenne, makes a fleeting appearance. His son

and heir, Henry, becomes ruler of High Lotharingia, and Henry's brother is Siegfried, founder of the House of Luxembourg.

Near the station at Trèves is an ancient building used as barracks. Of old it was an abbey, that of Saint Maximin, and his tomb. Vast lands belonged to it ; its revenue amounted to the enormous sum of from 80,000 to 100,000 ducats ; kings delighted to honour it ; queens showered gifts upon it ; the monks were known far and wide for their learning ; their library and treasures were priceless. Time has ruthlessly scattered all those glories ; the dust of those riches has been strewn between Madrid and Darmstadt. But in its time it was renowned as few abbeys have been, and to the tomb of St. Maximin pilgrims came in great numbers. Beggars and princes were among them, and one day Charles Martel, grandsire of Charlemagne, was carried and laid upon the tomb that he might be cured of his sickness. He recovered, and so grateful was he that he caused to be added to the domains of the monks the eastern portion of the great Merovingian Empire over which he ruled. In one of the districts of this territory was Lucilinburhut, as the Franks called it, the " little outpost," the name of which, changing first to Lutzelbourg, became our Luxembourg. It was this little outpost which Siegfried found — a small, decayed stronghold standing high in the air. He strengthened it and added greatly to it, and so began to appear that great fortress which saw perhaps more war than any other has seen between Gibraltar and Belgrade,

the desire to possess which drew the armies of more
than one king into the Duchy with unsheathed and
thirsty swords.

With Siegfried, first of a long line of spiritual
and temporal rulers and warriors, the story of feudal
Luxembourg opens. The line ran from the tenth
to the fifteenth century. Castles were built on all
the country's finest heights ; at their bases the little
villages of serfs grew in the shadow of the overlord's might. The size of the country grew, till it
was about half a dozen times larger than the Luxembourg we know to-day. But though the royal house
was powerful and comparatively enlightened, it was
seldom quite strong enough to hold the masters of
the castles of the land in proper leash. These nobles
played with their lands as a gambler plays with
coins. They sold and mortgaged and made presents
of their acres here, there and everywhere ; then
they fought to get them back, and sold them again
when treasure ran low. Of all the figures of this
period of the history of Luxembourg, the outstanding
personage is Jean l'Aveugle (John the Blind), Count
of Luxembourg and King of Bohemia, whose reign
was war, the universal provider of military strength,
the roving war-lord, whose life ended at Crécy, and
from whose helm the Black Prince tore the three
feathers with the motto, " Ich Dien," the heritage of
Princes of Wales to this day. John was a wanderer
in death as in life ; his bones were moved from
place to place almost as often as those of another
wanderer, Columbus.

His successor was Wenceslas, the first to assume

the title of Duke of Luxembourg, and for the first
time the country became a Duchy, to remain so till
to-day. Under him the country flourished, but, as
was so often the case in the history of old, good
work did not long survive its author. His nephew,
Wenceslas II, who followed him, saw in the fruits
of good government the wherewithal for dissipation,
and he created a record, a fairly hard thing to achieve
in those days, as wastrel, gambler and drunkard.
Not only did he undo all the good work of his uncle,
but he mortgaged the entire Duchy to a number of
different people. He had a niece, Elizabeth of
Görlitz, who had been promised by him a " dot " of
over 100,000 florins. He actually gave the oft-
pawned Duchy as security ! She signed over her
rights to her nephew, Philip of Burgundy, for an
immediate and an annually payable consideration.
In this curious transaction we see one of the foundations of the gigantic realm of Charles V which Philip
was beginning to hammer into being. He had to
fight for his aunt's gift. The people tried to hold the
Luxembourg citadel, but they failed. The Luxembourgers appealed to the Duke of Saxony, who was
coming to their aid, when a solid cash offer from
Philip bought him off.

The coming of Philip marks clearly and distinctly
the close of feudalism ; but Luxembourg's evil days
are far from being ended. Ambition was still to
stride across the Duchy with heavy footsteps and to
leave its traces red with blood and black with ruin ;
it was still to be for a lengthy time Might's tilting-
ground. Philip did not take the title of Duke of

Luxembourg, and his son Charles the Bold (one of whose wives was a sister of Edward IV of England) had to go and buy it from—the King of Poland ! That royal personage acquired it by marrying the daughter of Sigismund, one of the last rulers of Siegfried's line. Charles was warlike and bloodthirsty, and his wars soaked the Duchy in blood and tears. He left a daughter, whose marriage with the Archduke Maximilian transferred the country to the Austrian House. When Maximilian came to the throne he ridded himself of some parts of the wide realms over which he had dominion, and Luxembourg, Burgundy and the Netherlands became the domain of Philip, his son, who married Jeanne of Arragon and Castille. Their son, Charles, was given the title of Duke of Luxembourg, the first title of the glittering array of which Charles V was eventually to be able to boast, and Luxembourg was the first piece of earth over which there ruled that sovereign who was to sway the destinies of an empire outshining that of Rome. Though Luxembourg, under that Empire one of the United States of the Netherlands, was allowed to keep its own customs and laws and rule itself by means of a local council, it had little cause to rejoice that it belonged to the realm over which Charles ruled. Once again the Duchy became a battle-ground ; the Germans and the French wrought equal and awful havoc within its borders, and the now powerful fortress, the envy of all, lured armies to its conquest. Once it fell before the soldiery of the Dukes of Orleans and Guise, but the forces of Charles quickly took it from them again. War, too, made an additional drain upon the country. Towards the end of his reign Charles had an ever-increasing need for money, and he had no compassion for the little country which had stood so faithfully by him. He put heavy loads of taxation upon it, wringing his tolls most mercilessly from the people, adding religious persecution to the tortures he imposed.

An empire in which people were so treated was doomed to break up, and when Charles's son, Philip II, ruled, the inevitable split came. North and South Netherlands ranged against each other and across the Duchy, which remained faithful to Philip, he hurled his avalanches of Spanish and German troops against the rebellious north. Luxembourg was once more one great field of war. Under the viceroyalty of Albert of Austria, who had married Philip's daughter, the struggle continued with unabated fury. Then a little more than a decade of peace intervened, and after that the Thirty Years' War broke out. It is not necessary to recount here all the horrors of that gigantic struggle—one of the most hideous in the whole of the history of Europe or the world. Death, ruin, torture, famine and pestilence garnered frightful harvests, and all these terrors appeared to reach their height in and around Luxembourg. However many people were slaughtered, however many towns and villages were razed to the ground, war and all its attendant woes could not wipe out Luxembourg. Its citizens were made of stern stuff, of the hard, imperishable material from which real nations are cast.

Peace came, and the Duchy remained part of the Empire of Charles V, the greatness of which was fast ebbing. Spain and Germany waned ; Louis the Fourteenth's ambitions were soon reddening and blackening many fair lands, and he coveted another— Luxembourg. Into the Duchy he sent the redoubtable Marshal Boufflers, who dealt sternly with castle after castle. The marks of his visitation are still to be seen to-day on many a wall. When the resistance of the Duchy had been weakened by this method, siege was laid to the capital, and after an investment of a little more than a month the Spanish garrison surrendered the place. Under the great " Sun King " there was peace for a while and fair prosperity ; but Louis did not believe in the little Duchy's retaining its rights and privileges, and these he cut away. In spite, however, of that denial of nationality, Luxembourg flourished. But when Louis was faced by the formidable combination of England, Spain, Holland and Germany, the whole gamut of the horror of war and disorder was experienced once again. Peace found the country taken from France ; the Spanish returned with all the evils of misgovernment and tyranny, and a Dutch garrison was set down in the fortress of Luxembourg's capital. Then Austria and France quarrelled over the Spanish succession on the death of the weak Charles II. The Elector of Bavaria, who possessed himself of the citadel of Luxembourg, made a bid to win the Netherlands, and added fuel to the fire. All that concerns us here, however, is that he was only partially successful, and the Treaty of

LUXEMBOURG : HIGH TOWN AND SUBURB OF GRUND.

To face p. 32.

Utrecht robbed him even of the little he gained, and handed our Duchy over to Austria. That was a surprise, but it also turned out to be a very considerable blessing. It gave, in the first place, peace to a war-racked land for over three-quarters of a century, a period of time in which Austria made a laudable effort to set the feet of the Luxembourgers firmly on their mother earth. They were quick to take advantage of the respite and the opportunities it presented, and prosperity and progress, not only material, were the result under the fairly genial reforming influences of Austria, guided by Charles VI, Marie Thérèse, and, to some extent, by Joseph II, who was somewhat too hard on the religious orders for Luxembourg's taste.

But great historic events were soon to turn the thoughts of Luxembourg from domestic affairs and from the strengthening of its nationality. From the paths of peace it was quickly and roughly called back again to the ways of war. The French Revolution broke out. Everything quickly fell before the relentless forces of the Republic, but Luxembourg's fortress held out from the end of October 1794 until the beginning of June 1795, when its ten thousand defenders gave way before the stern enemy, Famine. The unpoetic revolutionaries labelled the Duchy after its annexation to the Republic "Le Département des Forêts"! Whatever "Liberté, Egalité, Fraternité" meant elsewhere, they, as the Republicans interpreted them in conquest, made Luxembourg a hell. All the more hideous were the extortions and rapacities of the French, seeing that

they came after a long era of peace in which the
Luxembourgers had outlived the horrors of war and
oppression. The most awful of tyrannies were in-
dulged in by the so-called emissaries of the latest
freedom and the rights of man. The country was
goaded into revolution, and the brave but ill-starred
Peasants' War was the result. It was repressed in
a wild orgy of the most heartless cruelty, but at
least the fiery spirit of the people drew Napoleon's
admiration.

The French Empire rose and went quickly to its
ruin. The Congress of Vienna carved out Europe
anew, and did it badly. Belgium and Holland
became the kingdom of William I. That monarch
was stripped of Nassau, which became Prussian, and
received the Grand Duchy of Luxembourg in return
for it ; the Grand Duchy became at the same time
part of the German Confederation, with a Prussian
garrison in Luxembourg—a most absurd arrangement ; all east of Our, Sure and Mosel was handed
over to Prussia, some compensation being given to
the Duchy on the opposite border. But the re-
arrangement was not final. The Belgians rose in
revolt, and from 1830 to 1839 everything was in
disorder. Belgium and Holland settled their differ-
ences by the Treaty of London, and at the same time
Luxembourg's final shape upon the map was decided.
Whenever the province's bounds have been fixed, that
process has been accomplished by cutting pieces off
it. And so it was on this occasion. What we now
know as Belgian Luxembourg was given to Belgium,
and the result of that geographical operation was

the Grand Duchy of Luxembourg as the map of Europe shows it to-day.

Only once more was there to be a war alarm before the country settled down to that prosperity and contentedness which peace alone can bring, to that happiness which is achieved by making no history. When the German Confederation fell in 1866, the Prussians did not withdraw their garrison placed in Luxembourg when the Congress of Vienna handed it over in "a sort of" way to the Confederation. This annoyed France, which also thought that she had some very considerable right to the country, seeing that Prussia had been having so much of her own way elsewhere in the matter of territory. But, replied Prussia, the Duchy is more akin to Germany than France. The dispute brought the nations, so soon to meet in the deadly struggle of '70, to the verge of war. But the battle-cloud did not burst ; the Powers settled the matter by making the Duchy an independent and neutral State and deciding that the fortifications of the capital should be razed. And so it was. The Prussian garrison marched home again, and under the supervision of a French and a Prussian officer the noble walls of the great citadel were clumsily blown to bits. The long ages of warfare were over ; the coming of the final peace was celebrated by felling the towers of as proud a fortress as the god of war ever rejoiced over. Grass and moss climb up over the ruins, roses grow on the grim redans, trees there are instead of towers —Luxembourg's fighting days are a memory ; " the curtains of yesterday drop down, the curtains of to-morrow roll up " ; and let us hope that the alchemy of peace will never again be interrupted in its beneficent processes.

Yet the arrangement which robbed Luxembourg of its seductive fortress did not come a moment too soon. As the last turrets of the citadel were blasted, away to the south the guns rumbled ; France and Germany were opening their great trial of strength of 1870. But this time the waves of war did not sweep over Luxembourg. Since then the Grand Duchy has but a short story to tell. On the death of William III, King of the Netherlands, in 1890, Adolf, Duke of Nassau, by virtue of a family pact, became Grand Duke of independent Luxembourg. He reigned till 1905, when his son William succeeded him. The Grand Duke William died in February 1912, leaving seven daughters, and now the eldest, Marie Louise Adelheid, who came of age shortly after her father's death, is Grand Duchess of Luxembourg. Such is the long ordeal through which the people of Luxembourg and their country have passed. I doubt if any other land can set forth one equally terrible or drawn out to such a length.

These great trials have left a people to-day hardy, progressive, hospitable and honest. They are hard-working too. Prosperity reigns, and in the Duchy now there is very little poverty, and one never meets a beggar. No class distinctions reign in the land, and the people are extremely religious. They may be, to those from great countries, big cities and daily, almost hourly, newspapers, old-fashioned in thought, and superstitious, but one cannot help seeing that, whatever Roman Catholicism has done elsewhere, it has certainly had no evil effects in our delectable Duchy. To be fair, of course, Roman Catholicism is often blamed for what a southern climate is really responsible. In Luxembourg the climate is all that can be desired ; the summer is delightful, the winter neither too long nor too severe. So we get a people sturdy in mind and body, children of Nature, upright and pure, believing in dreams and prayer, and, living in a romantic land, fond of endless tales of fairies and of their folk-lore, saint-worshippers, happy in the sun, bidding it good morning and good night with prayer.

But they are not at all a bigoted people. Consider this, remembering that at least 99 per cent. of them are Roman Catholics, and, what is more, extremely devout Catholics. Last year an Education Bill was brought forward in Parliament by the Liberal-Socialist " Bloc." That measure had the effect of making religious instruction to all intents and purposes optional and dependent on the wish of the parent. In the giving of that instruction a good deal more responsibility was thrown upon the priests. They rose against the Bill, using the whole force of their matchless organization to stir up sufficient opposition to kill it. But no : the people, convinced that the measure would be a useful one, would not be stirred. It went through Parliament, and then came before the Grand Duchess for signature. And it was in this instance that Luxembourg's young ruler gave evidence that she is going to be a constitutional ruler at all costs. There can be no doubt that all the pressure of the Roman Catholic Church was brought to bear upon her to veto the measure. The power of that influence may be gauged by the fact that had the Grand Duchess's mother still been regent, as she was till but a month or two earlier, the Bill, it is said, would never have become law. Yet the Grand Duchess, without hesitation, signed it. A Sunday or two later, from every pulpit came fulminations against " la nouvelle loi scolaire," and some were bold enough to hurl thinly disguised threats against the Grand Duchess herself. The Church announced that it would refuse to work under the Act. But Luxembourg refused to be greatly moved ; the Grand Duchy stood by the law and its young Queen. The Grand Duchess had just previously given proof that she takes her high duties seriously, and does not intend to be a mere figurehead. One of her first acts after she took the reins of power was to recall a measure which had been vetoed during the short regency and give it her sanction !

Beautiful, highly educated, simple in her tastes, devoted to her work and her country, the Grand Duchess is adored by her people. They worship her all the more because she is so thoroughly Luxembourgian at heart. During the two previous reigns German influence was supreme at Court. That accounts for the great inroads which the Germans made in all directions in the Grand Duchy. But under the young Queen that is so no more, and to be Luxembourger is not now a drawback. Worth, not a German name or title, wins its way at the

simply conducted yet enlightened Court of the Grand
Duchy. It has pleased the people immensely that
the young ruler has shown herself so thoroughly
patriotic, despite the strong influences which must
demand a deviation from the path at times. Long
may the Grand Duchess rule over her beautiful
Ruritania !

The people, of course, are mainly agriculturists,
and in perhaps no other country is such great attention paid to the culture of the soil. Agricultural
instruction is an extremely important part of education, and the Government renders every possible
assistance to the people. " Agriculture," said a
prominent Luxembourg authority to me, " is really
several sciences in one. It would be absurd to think
that the best can be got out of the land unless those
who work it are properly trained and can have,
when it is necessary, the most up-to-date advice
on every possible point. We endeavour to live up
to those two maxims. If a man's land is poor we
put it right for him ; if he wants stock we obtain
it for him from the best sources and provide him
with it at the lowest possible figure, giving, wherever
required, most liberal credit. The advanced state
of agriculture shows that that policy is highly
successful, and its progress is of enormous value to
the country and to the people. We pay great attention, too, to afforestation ; yet, as you know, the
scenery in our little country loses none of its natural
charm—does not look in the slightest degree ' made '
or artificial. In no country in the world, I believe,
are those who intend to devote themselves to agri-

culture so well and carefully educated, and nowhere is the path before them made so smooth. That education is not at all expensive—in fact, I think I may say that nowhere is it so cheap ; and we have people who come even from England to take advantage of our educational system, not only in its agritural branches but in all its stages. To such, of course, training is somewhat more expensive than it is to the native-born, but still cheaper than almost anywhere else in Europe. And after a pupil has finished his educational course he does not find his way barred or difficult owing to conditions of land tenure such as exist in other countries. Here we have no land hunger, for the land really 'belongs to the people. There are no great estates held up by wealthy landlords, and from the State or the commune land can be obtained, can be purchased or rented. Our law of succession, too, prevents large holdings from remaining in one hand and being probably neglected, or at least not developed as fully as possible. Property is not left entirely to an eldest son, but must be equally divided amongst all the children. We have therefore no younger sons, or daughters for that matter, forced to abandon the land. On the death of their father all find themselves in possession of a plot of land, and if it is small so much greater is the stimulus given to cultivate it to the best advantage. And it is never difficult to add to it if desired."

So the little Grand Duchy flourishes. It does not waste its strength on the vain things, but applies it to the things which count. It is about the most serious little nation that exists, and yet no country is happier. An all-sufficing simplicity reigns, and long may the unsettling factors of a restless civilization halt at its borders and leave it with its lowlier ways, which lead most surely to all that is best in nationhood. That the sunbeams of success and content will long brighten those paths will be the ardent wish of all those who wander by its heights and plains and valleys, and learn to know its people, who are akin in so much to ourselves—a delightful land, in which

> You shall be lost, and learn
> New being, and forget
> The world, till your return
> Shall bring your first regret.

THE CAPITAL OF THE GRAND DUCHY

A rose-red city, half as old as Time.

J. W. BURGON.

CHAPTER II

THE CAPITAL OF THE GRAND DUCHY

THE most devout worshipper of the open road will find it difficult to tear himself away from Luxembourg's capital, even after he has wandered through it from end to end and seen everything there is to see. The little city has a lure all its own. Beauty, with her deft fingers, and Romance, with her long and patient toil, have done their work with infinite pains and a delightful completeness of collaboration. It requires art to set a fortress down in fairyland without outraging all the proprieties ; yet here it has been done, and if Romance now rests upon her weighty laurels Beauty still works on, tirelessly spinning her web over the works of war. Those fair partners have, perhaps, nowhere else in Europe worked together with such delightful effect. The little city has aspects endlessly new, a subtle, compelling charm which will fast breed in the most confirmed country-lover Charles Lamb's "low urban taste."

The upper town is high "in Sonne und Luft," on a great rock, on three sides of which two demure little streams, aided, it may be, by some power of the underworld, have cut deep fosses. Under the sheltering height the low town nestles, while high over it runs a network of imposing viaducts. The tiny Petrusse, a filmy, silken thread of a river, having all to itself a vale which the Thames might now and again envy, twists round the southern side of the high town. From the opposite direction comes the Alzette, into whose valley powder-mill and cloth factory have crept. The little Petrusse marries the Alzette in quietest bridal and takes its name, and the river sweeps along the eastern side of the citadel in a huge S, through which the railway sends the dollar sign. Heights look across the valley at heights ; fortresses, which once grinned at one another with their teeth of cannon, now share an equal peace and are one in their powerlessness. Luxembourg, once the inland Gibraltar, is a little peaceful city of infinite loveliness, retaining all the best of what the years have bestowed, and constantly renewing its youth.

If it was an inland Gibraltar, it is now another Bruges, with its bridged ravines and rivers. It has more than a touch of Bruges and something beyond a mere tinge of Benares. It retains the marks of its conquerors. Buildings are to be seen which an Austrian must have built ; others proclaim clearly that their architects had something in them of the spirit of those who reared the Alhambra and Burgos Cathedral. Then down in the low town the people live as they must have lived in the reign of Charlemagne. Narrow ruelles and age-old dwellings recall a long past. Dim twilight there carries one back to the time of Siegfried, and makes one see a primi-

LUXEMBOURG: GENERAL VIEW.

To face p. 49.

tive world. Fading day, too, makes even more impressive that towering, ruined citadel which in its day was menaced by the "iron chard" now of Spaniard and German, now of Frenchman and Austrian, and held by all in turn. And during the long summer days how beautiful is this flower-city !— for so it is, resplendent with its roses, for which Luxembourg is so justly famous far and wide. The visitor becomes almost convinced that this old fortress has now a nature-lover for governor. It is "roses, roses all the way." How that Eve in the Aztec's Garden of Eden would have been tempted by those Gloires de Dijon, climbing many a wall in all their glory of buff and yellow, orange and fawn ! Then there are proud Maréchals, certainly in place in an ancient fortress—Maréchal Niel, splendid in yellow regimentals, and Maréchal Vaillant, in full-dress crimson. Along rose-scented alleys the large golden balls of a Cloth of Gold Noisette bloom shyly in the glorious summer days ; many paths are painted in the paradise colours of scarlet and white and tender pink by Provence, Bourbon, Scotch, Tuscany, Damask and Chinese tea roses. Luxembourg has indeed much for the rose-lover, and is the home of many delightful old rose-growers, men of the order of most ancient gentlemen—gardeners, ditchers and grave-diggers. Trees and terraces top the dizzy walls, and where once the grim, bare battlements frowned mosses spread ever wider and wider their soft, fadeless carpets.

Goethe, in October 1792, made a short stay in Luxembourg, which charmed him greatly. In his

" Memoirs " he speaks of its grandeur, its gravity
and its grace. The Monks' Vale, Pfaffenthal, he
calls " a pledge of peace and rest, though every
look upwards recalls war and violence and ruin."
" Luxembourg," he added, " resembles nothing but
itself." And that is true. Life in the little city
goes very peacefully and pleasantly. With its 23,000
inhabitants, it is perhaps the most prosperous town
there is of its size. It is, of course, a capital, with
its Court and Government departments, and these
alone give it a definite position of importance. But
it is not content with that. Factories of various
kinds dot the lower town, and year by year the upper
town looks across the ravines to see new streets
and buildings spreading themselves farther and still
farther to the south and to the west. The little city,
once oppressed and circumscribed by the limits of
a fortress, has grown enormously in the genial atmosphere of peace.

Luxembourg used to possess a most miserable
little railway station, which gave visitors the worst
possible first impression. They had to carry their
luggage to where the carriages in which to drive up
to the town might or, far more probably, might
not be. A long wait was generally the rule., But
now all that has been changed. There are porters
and public vehicles in plenty, and the station has
been entirely rebuilt on a generous scale, the architect
having skilfully adapted eighteenth-century German
style to fit in with modern requirements. The new
station, too, has an excellent restaurant and a chef
with whose art Colonel Newnham-Davis would find
no fault.

The station is at the extremity of the new suburb of Hollerich, a rapidly rising part of the city, with many fine buildings, standing upon what is known as the Bourbon Plateau, an extensive eminence cut off from the old town by the Petrusse ravine. In ancient times the plateau was strongly fortified, and from near the station it is said that a subterranean passage ran to the Bock, the chief part of the citadel of old. The Mercier Champagne Company utilize a large part of these old underground excavations for storing their stocks of wine, and an application by a visitor who wishes to see those ancient casements will meet with a prompt and generous permission. Four million bottles of champagne are generally stored there.

In driving to the upper town from the station, a drive of a mile or so, the visitor should instruct his driver to go via the new Avenue de la Liberté, so as to enter the town at its most picturesque spot. At the end of the thoroughfare are two magnificent buildings—one the headquarters of the Crédit Foncier Luxembourgeois, and the other the offices of the Chemins de Fer d'Alsace-Lorraine. They face the handsome new Adolf Bridge, completed in the summer of 1903 at a cost of 1,500,000 francs, and built by M. Séjourné, the engineer whose great feat was the Paris-Lyon-Mediterranean Railway. It crosses the deep Petrusse valley in a single stone span, 260 feet in length and 135 feet in height—the largest of its kind in the world. The workmanship, in Sure freestone, is delightfully graceful. From the bridge a magnificent view of the town is obtained,

4

and also of the prettily laid-out park deep down on the banks of the Petrusse.

From a little beyond the bridge to the west, on the far side of the Avenue Marie Thérèse, lies the City Park. It is officially so called, but the people do not forget that it runs, a semicircle of silver, from the Petrusse first north and then west to the Alzette, over the ground where brave Luxembourgers often stood desperately at bay behind the fort's strong walls. So it is, popularly, called the "Jardin du Général," for here the commander of the forces of old no doubt cultivated a pretty little patch of garden amid the sombre surroundings of war. The park stretches just like the border of a huge, embroidered fan, and from the centre of the high town handsome streets radiate through it. It was in 1872, a couple of years after the overthrow of the fortifications, that it was decided to lay out the park. Not a little of the beauty of the Côte d'Azur is evident, for the work was carried out by M. Edouard André, who designed the gardens of Monte Carlo, and his work here took fifteen years to complete. Plants and flowers in surprising variety are everywhere ; the turf is exquisite ; there are shady trees and pretty little vales. From the rough ruins of the fortress walls the designer of the garden-park has produced the order of varied beauty. Between the Avenue Marie Thérèse and the Avenue Monterey is a well-kept botanical garden, and a little farther on is the Villa Louvigny. This is a restaurant, standing in the most picturesquely rugged part of the park, where in warlike days was one of the bastions of

IN THE PFAFFENTHAL, LUXEMBOURG.

this imposing redoubt, which, garbed in the beauty of peace, is still haunted by flickering snatches of warlike memories. The proprietor of the restaurant will show visitors the subterranean passages here. This delightful spot is much frequented in summer by the Luxembourgers, and concerts, and frequent cycle races, too, are held in the evenings. By pleasant pathways the tour of the Jardin du Général can be made, and it is a delightful walk, ending, near the Pescatore Institute, at a terrace from which a magnificent view of the Pfaffenthal Clausen, the Bock and the valley of the Eisch spreads before the eyes.

The Pescatore Institute is a large and handsome four-story building standing in pretty grounds of about twelve acres in extent. It is a haven for any descendants of the founder or any citizen of Luxembourg who may fall upon bad times. M. Jean Pierre Pescatore, who had been Minister of the Netherlands in Paris, left, on his death in 1853, a sum of half a million francs for the purpose of founding such an institute, with the provision that the work was not to be commenced until the money, lying at compound interest, had doubled itself, thus ensuring that there should be ample funds to set the refuge on such a financial basis as would make certain that it could be carried on upon an adequate and generous scale. The park in which is the Pescatore Institute is the highest part of the plateau on which Luxembourg stands. It towers high above the Pfaffenthal and the Alzette, and affords an extensive vista over the heights on the opposite side of the river. A beauti-

fully green wooded slope, cut by paths, leads down
to the left bank of the stream.

A view of a different kind greets the visitor who
enters the town by the south-eastern side instead
of the south-western. Following the Avenue de la
Gare, the upper town is reached by a fine viaduct
over the Petrusse. It has twenty-five arches, the
highest having a height of about 130 feet. On the
left the visitor looks up the stream to the Adolf
Bridge and down upon the prettily laid-out grounds
by the Petrusse's banks. On the right is a lovely
view of part of the lower town and the Alzette valley.
Luxembourg, indeed, is a " ville de viaducs," having
a mile and a half of them altogether. To carry
the railway along the eastern side of the town three
viaducts are necessary, the largest of which is about
half a mile long, with forty-two arches, thirteen of
which are over 150 feet high.

The upper town is most romantic and interesting.
Many of the streets are old and narrow ; others,
broad and new. Some buildings are in the latest
styles of architecture ; others recall the stormy
history of city and duchy. Yet old and new blend
admirably. Nothing that the latest generations have
erected looks at all out of place in a city the lustre
of which must always be that of the past. Where
modernity is most in evidence, Luxembourg looks like
a little Brussels. It would be interesting to know
what proportion of the population consists of bakers,
and how many people have jewellery shops, for bakery
and jewellery establishments strike the visitor as being
extraordinarily numerous for a place of its size. The

new-comer who wishes to buy some of the delightful cakes which the bakers of the city produce should be warned that they are baked early in the week ; the people buy them on Thursdays or Fridays to consume on Saturdays or Sundays. On Friday, therefore, they are scarce, and a Saturday's quest is hopeless. Luxembourg has an important open-air market held in the Place Guillaume II, the roomy square which is the centre of the city from the point of view of the visitor, for in its neighbourhood are all the " Sehenswürdigkeiten." The peasants of the Duchy, as seen at market, are a particularly high type, well dressed, clean, good-looking, intelligent and straightforward in their dealings. In this particular market is a peculiar feature. All eggs are divided into two classes. At one spot I noticed a big sign which read : " Place pour la vente des œufs frais." At another part this was the legend : " Place pour la vente des œufs conservés." I am afraid that all market authorities do not take such great care to guard the rights of the egg-eater !

The Place Guillaume is the largest in the town. In the centre is the equestrian statue of William II, King of the Netherlands, erected in 1884, the highly decorative work of Antonin Mercié. William, who was the Prince of Orange present at the battle of Waterloo, is represented as entering Luxembourg— the occasion was in 1842—and responding to the enthusiastic reception given him by his subjects who so warmly and loyally admired him. And they had much to thank him for. To celebrate the visit commemorated by the statue he gave the Luxembourgers many of their rights, including their franchise laws, which they still enjoy to-day. The pedestal has the coats of arms of the cantons of the Duchy.

On the south side of the square is the heavily imposing Hôtel de Ville, which, commenced in 1830, was not finished for fourteen years. It contains the Pescatore Museum in the " grande salle " on the first floor, a handsome hall used by the deputies as their place of meeting from 1848 to 1860. Here a large collection of French and Dutch pictures and objets d'art awaits a more suitable and a permanent home. But though these have only a temporary abiding-place in the Hôtel de Ville, the visitor cannot help thinking that it would be worth while to place the exhibits in at least some sort of order. Nothing is shown off to advantage. The exhibits constitute another of M. Pescatore's benefactions. He bequeathed to Luxembourg all the art treasures which decorated his Paris and St. Cloud residences, treasures which had been acquired by large purchases from the collections of William II, Louis Philippe and others. There are about a hundred old and modern pictures, including water-colours by Décamps, Prud'hon, Charlet, Callow, Cattermole and Horace Vernet, sketches by Marc and Clerget, pastels by Vidal, etchings and numerous works in marble and bronze. It is an extremely creditable " one-man collection," and many of the works of art which it contains are of considerable value. In the museum is also the collection given to the municipality by M. Lippmann, an eminent Amsterdam banker.

From the eastern side of the Place Guillaume a

GRAND DUCAL PALACE, LUXEMBOURG.

To face p. 55.

short street, the rue de la Reine,[1] leads to the rue de Gouvernement, on the far side of which stands the Grand Ducal Palace. It is an exceedingly beautiful building, though the narrow streets by which it is surrounded do not permit of the full extent of its delicate charm being effectively displayed. It is entered direct from the street, no gardens surrounding it, and has a noble simplicity most strikingly in keeping with an unpretentious people and also with their splendid past. Interior and exterior both tell Luxembourg's story ; the art of brush and chisel and needle deck it. It was Count Ernest of Mansfeld, Philip II's favourite, who, in 1572-3, built it in Spanish Renaissance style. It is certainly a tribute to the art and taste of the age, and, despite frequent enlargements and renovations, its original beauty, inside and out, has been very carefully preserved. The outer walls are decorated with delicate arabesques in bas-relief, and at each side of the front a hexagonal tower, of light and perfect design, rises from the first floor. The two towers are joined by a balcony of ironwork. Since the time of the Grand Duke Adolf buildings in the neighbourhood have been cleared away to permit of extensions, and the interior has been renovated on a princely scale. Entering from the rue de Gouvernement, a grand staircase leads to the elegant apartments on the first floor. The

[1] All names of places in Luxembourg are in French and German. Sometimes the French one is in common use, as in Jardin du Général, sometimes the German, as in Pfaffenthal. I invariably use that in more common use.

stair is a superb piece of work, its harmony of
line and great width compensating for the lack of
height and the somewhat crowded decoration general
in the age from which it dates. The grand salons
on the first floor contain full-length portraits in oils
of the Grand Dukes, heads of the House of Nassau,
and the State dining-room, which looks out on the
court at the rear, is hung with priceless Gobelin
tapestries depicting scenes from the Odyssey. On
the exterior of the palace there are relics which
tell us of bygone ages, of memorable events and
historical local happenings. Under a small door,
in the entrance hall leading to the court, may be
seen the monograms of Siegfried, the founder of
the city, and of the good Countess Ermesinde. She,
tradition has it, was the daughter of Melusina, the
Undine of the Alzette, who, taking human shape,
impersonated the consort of Henry IV. It was
Ermesinde who first gave the city its municipal freedom, and she did much in addition to further its
prosperity. One of the stones supporting the balcony
has upon it the Cross of Burgundy or of St. André ;
it dates from the time of Burgundy's supremacy in
the land, and also contains the jewel of the Golden
Fleece. Inscriptions are numerous. On one side
of the façade there is one extolling the merits of
the Count of Mansfeld, doubtless a self-performed
task ! On the wall at the rear of the older portion
of the palace there are to be seen bas-reliefs of
the ornamented casques of Henry VII and of Jean
l'Aveugle. Below that of Henry is his motto,
" Judicate Juste." Under the familiar one of Jean

is " Ich dien." Another inscription is " Libertate Prosperitas," appropriately enough below the carved head of Countess Ermesinde. Melusina is also there in relief.

The palace has had some illustrious guests in its time. Louis XIV stayed there in 1687. Racine was one of his suite. Napoleon I, in 1804, remained there for several days. It is open to view by the public when the Grand Ducal family is absent. The Chamber of Deputies continues the frontage of the palace. But with what a change ! In passing to it the eye goes from grace to Gothic tastelessness, from art to artifice. It is a modern building, built in 1857, and I hope Luxembourg will not perpetrate any more such eyesores.

In face of the Chamber of Deputies ends the rue Nicolas, the chief building in which is the Hôtel du Gouvernement, a massive structure in Renaissance style, which need not detain the explorer. The street leads into the rue de Notre Dame, where, on the left, rises one of the finest and most interesting buildings of the city—Notre Dame Cathedral, commonly called by the people the Church of St. Nicolas. Built during the latter part of the sixteenth century and the earlier part of the seventeenth, it was, together with some of the buildings which surround it, a convent of the Jesuits, and is reared on the spot where stood an ancient Franciscan convent. The magnificent old church has several remarkable features, and probably the first of which the visitor will learn is the extraordinary chime of bells. The bells are contained in a tower of most beautiful proportions, and every quarter of an hour they ring out a number of chords of Luxembourg airs and well-known folk-songs. The bells are most delightfully toned. Rising on high above the city, the tower was very often a mark for the guns of the besiegers in Luxembourg's long warlike times. The marks of cannon-balls are still noticeable on the tower, as they are on the beautiful façade, especially on the tympanum which carries the Spanish coat of arms. The portal is a perfect piece of Renaissance work. Two gracefully carved pillars on either side and statues, niches and arabesques are combined with really exquisite taste. On the left as one enters rises the cenotaph of Jean l'Aveugle. It is surrounded by a group of four life-size Biblical figures, and carries this inscription :—

D.O.M hoc sub altare
servatur Joannes, Rex
Bohemiae, Comes luxem
burgensis, Henrici
VII imperatoris filius,
Caroli IV, imperatoris pater,
Wenceslai et Sigismundi
imperatorum avus, princeps
animo maximus, obiit
MCCCXL, 30 Aug.

The inscription is, of course, not now correct. After his death, at Crécy, the blind warrior-king was buried in the Church of St. John, in the suburb of Grund, in the lower town, and the monument now in the Cathedral was erected over his tomb. But, as I have already said, John was a wanderer in death as in life. In Luxembourg he had no fewer than four resting-places, and was disturbed in his fourth by the French when they stormed the city in 1795. These vandals carried away the remains of the king, which fell into the hands of one named Boch, a person who was sacrilegious enough to deposit them in his crockery-ware museum at Metlach on the Sarre ! They were eventually rescued from those surroundings, and King Frederick IV of Prussia had a mausoleum built to receive them, a grim little chapel hanging on the side of a towering rock looking down upon the twisting Sarre. There the bones of the blind hero of Crécy repose in, let us hope, a final resting-place. It was when the Church of St. John was demolished that the monument was transferred to the Cathedral.

Another interesting feature of the Cathedral is that it displays three distinct styles of architecture. The windows and arches are nearly all pointed ; the façade and the rostrum are Renaissance work ; and a Moorish " motif " is strikingly evident in the shafts of the columns. No other Jesuit church in the world has the third characteristic, which is probably accounted for by the fact that the architect responsible for some of the work was a Spanish Jesuit. A masterpiece of sixteenth-century Flemish Renaissance is the rood-screen with its particularly beautiful carving. The Moorish note is seen in the exquisite interlaced beading round the columns—work which is repeated round the arch of the choir. The frescoes in the choir are modern and represent scenes from the life of Jesus. All the three styles of architecture blend most harmoniously, and the whole effect is pleasing in the extreme. The Cathedral also contains a statue of the Virgin Mary, to which miraculous powers are attributed. Pilgrims and sufferers invoke it under the name of Consolatrix afflictorum, and many hundreds of them, and spectators as well, come to be present at its feast, which lasts from the fourth to the fifth Sunday after Easter. The Cathedral has many valuable treasures, among them being a perfectly preserved insignia of the Golden Fleece, a gorgeous chasuble, the gift of Count Ernest of Mansfeld, a robe for the statue of the Virgin Mary, woven and worked by Marie Thérèse herself. At the rear of the Cathedral is the Grand Seminary, a building which was originally part of the Jesuits' convent ; it has no interest, and it is even doubtful if it were ever actually used by the Jesuits as a seminary.

But the Cathedral does not exhaust the interest in the former convent buildings. Here, too, is to be found the Athénée, in a structure which has been put to many uses in its time. Not very long ago it was wholly occupied by the pupils, nearly one thousand in number, of the gymnasium and the industrial and commercial school, both of which institutions have become well known beyond Luxembourg's borders. The latter division, however, was lately removed to a modernly equipped building in the north-western suburb, Limpersburg. Now only the gymnasium pupils remain, and about half of them are housed in a hostel forming part of the cluster of buildings. Beautiful grounds are attached to the buildings, and any visitor interested in education will find no difficulty in his way if he wishes to see this excellent school at work. The National Library is also here. It consists of 80,000 volumes, many of them very old, and a large number of valuable manuscripts. Among the latter are the " Liber Epistolarum Guidoni de Bassochius " and the " Natural History of Pliny the Younger," dating from the eleventh century. A particularly interesting rarity is a book of prayers, decorated with fifteenth-century miniatures. The collection of natural history specimens to be seen here is also worth a visit, but more attractive still is the museum of antiquities, mainly of the Gallo-Roman epoch in Luxembourg. A complete series of the coins of the Duchy is exhibited. Behind all those edifices the boulevard which leads to the Petrusse viaduct spreads out into a spacious, tree-shaded " place "—La Place de la Constitution—an elevated embankment which provides a lovely coup d'œil up and down the Petrusse between the two bridges, a section of the river ravine which has won for itself by its charm the name of " Italy " from the people. Even in the winter the cold winds seem to wander wide from this secluded little vale which the mighty artist Nature ever decks with her most delicate and ever-changing robes of colour, a wonderful contrast to the town above it, " all spired and domed and turreted." On the promenade overlooking this part of the river valley all Luxembourg delights to stroll and chat while enjoying the music provided by the military band during summer evenings. Another such place is the Place d'Armes, not far from the Place Guillaume. There is music there on three evenings of the week, and on two sides of the square are cafés and restaurants in profusion. The little city is certainly not overcrowded with institutions to provide amusement. Not a single music-hall exists, and the municipal theatre—once a church !— is open but for a short winter season, when Court and Society are at home. Last year I discovered a couple of good, if modest, cinematograph theatres in dim, narrow streets in the neighbourhood of the palace. A much-favoured institution in Luxembourg is the Casino, situated at the end of the rue Aldringer, and with a spacious terrace looking out on the valley of the Petrusse. In this " club " is undoubtedly the best restaurant in the city and a large and well-equipped reading-room. Concerts and lectures are frequently given, and the visitor may have the use of the Casino after the slight formality of being introduced by a member. Any one wishing to have more than the ordinary tourist's knowledge of Luxembourg and its people should certainly take advantage of the introduction into society offered through the Casino.

To return for a little to the Place d'Armes, the visitor should see there the delightfully artistic monument which was in 1903 erected to the memory of two of Luxembourg's national poets, Lentz and Dicks. At the foot of a graceful column, a girl crowns the heads, in bas-relief, with garlands, while a young worker sings Lentz's national hymn— " Feierwôn." It is, by the way, the music of the

THE BOCK, LUXEMBOURG.

To face p. 63.

refrain of that hymn which the bells of the Cathedral ring out every alternate hour. Round the column is the first line of the words of the refrain, carved in the stone. They are in the Luxembourg patois, and mean : " We wish to remain just as we are." Luxembourg desires to be left alone in peace to work out her destiny, and the way in which those two poets inculcated this quiet patriotism and glorified the Luxembourg spirit has ensured them a place in the Duchy's heart for ever. On the top of the column a lion holds the Luxembourg arms. The monument is the work of a skilled young artist, Federspiel.

Of late years Luxembourg has been lavish in the erection of public buildings. Opposite the poets' monument is the Palais Municipal, the façade of which is also Federspiel's work, and a bas-relief shows Luxembourg's citizens receiving their charter of liberty from the Countess Ermesinde. The Post Office, newly completed, in the rue du Génie, is another fine building ; and not far away is the Synagogue, a beautiful building in Moorish-Byzantine style. Banks are responsible for several striking improvements, and the commercial houses of the Grand' Rue are one by one being rebuilt, so that soon the rue de la Paix of Luxembourg should be a most handsome thoroughfare.

There are many ways from the upper town to the lower, but before exploring that part of Luxembourg which is huddled closely down by the lazy Alzette, the Bock, the cradle of the city, should be visited.

This curious rock—the barrel of the pistol with which the fortress met its foes—juts out into the northern curve of the river from the oldest part of the upper town. No other citadel in the world has seen so much of war, and few are so rich in clusters of romance which Time has bestowed. Siegfried and Jean l'Aveugle had their castles here ; ruler after ruler, race after race added to its strength, and remnants of the work of all remain. An ivy-hung tower, the only one out of seven that still stands, and deep wells in the rock carry us back to pre-Conquest times, when history and romance blend delightfully. Who was this Siegfried round whose name the years have spun a legend as of that of Lohengrin reversed? Let me first tell the story as Romance will have it, and then see what the investigators make of it. Siegfried married the most beautiful Melusina, who, having a horrible secret, would only consent to the marriage on a certain condition. That was that on one certain day of the year he should leave her free, and should not attempt to see her during the twenty-four hours. He agreed, being doubtless warned that if he attempted, and was successful in, an evasion of the stipulation all happiness would come to an end with startling suddenness. Whatever there was supernatural about the beautiful bride, Siegfried was distressingly human. When the short " close season " arrived he endeavoured to learn his beautiful wife's secret, and it was revealed to him as he peered through a keyhole. Startled to see the fair one in mermaid shape, the astonished man uttered, as well he might, a loud cry of surprise, which told Melusina that her secret was " out." That spell, which gave her human shape for all but one day of the year, was broken, and the beautiful mermaid dived into the nearest domain of suitable element—the Alzette.

Romance gives the story variety—a habit which Romance has. One variant is that Melusina vowed that she would sew a garment, taking seven years for every stitch, and that when the piece of work was finished Luxembourg's doom would fall upon it without warning. Roughly, she must have put in something like a hundred and fifty stitches by now, so that the city may safely count upon a fairly long span of life yet, judging by the intricate needle-work of the time. Another story is that the spell was to break and allow the lovely prisoner of the water to return to the world of humans when a certain number of rulers had been born of Siegfried's line. With Henry IV the number was completed and the spell broke again, with the result that the event mentioned earlier in this chapter took place. No wonder Melusina is regarded as the protectress of the city ! But still another story has it that Melusina has not yet left her Alzette, fay-guarded abode. She is said to appear once every hundred years, seeking for a bold cavalier to break the spell. Then she comes at night in the guise of a hideous, terror-striking serpent, and in her mouth she carries the key of the city. If any one meets her and is bold enough to take the key from her mouth Melusina is free, and no doubt the hero's reward will be the fair one's hand in marriage—let us hope without the

5

temptation which beset poor Siegfried ! And just
as there are people who have seen the sea-serpent,
so there are those who have seen Melusina in this
repulsive form, but none has been bold enough to
secure the key. Sometimes when revels are held in
the vaults of the Bock, merrymakers declare they
have seen the apparition. But, as the somewhat
matter-of-fact Luxembourger who shows visitors over
the Bock caves says, that only goes to prove that
they *are* merrymakers !

The Alzette Melusina has, of course, more than one
" double " in the wide realms of romance, and when
the stern modern searcher after truth has done with
the story it has undergone considerable modification,
not, however, sufficient to leave it without interest.
One of those explorers would have us believe that
Siegfried is no less a personage than Hercules.
Luxembourg was a spot consecrated for the veneration of this hero. Siegfried of the Rhine was one
and the same divinity, to whom the greater river
has no substantial claim. Therefore it follows that
Luxembourg is the real classic ground of the
Nibelungen ! If I felt inclined to do a little
amateur exploration of this kind, I would set out to
prove that the legend is much more likely to have
come up from the Rhine than to have floated down
to it. But, in this place at least, I must, with the
tact of the appreciative guest, desist from such work
and give Luxembourg the full benefit of every doubt.
As for Melusina, the authority I have quoted insists
that she is none other than " la grande Diane arden-
naise." As a lover of Luxembourg, again I like to

think that from the delectable little Duchy went forth all the legends which cluster round the name of that fair divinity. And there may be something in the idea, for if the wanderer, when at Echternach, crosses the river and enters the woods any one will guide him to a crumbling, broken altar, upon which he can read :

> Deae Dianae
> Q Postumius
> Potens V S [1]

Only I wish some clever person would make the dates connected with Siegfried (of Luxembourg) and Hercules, with Melusina and Diana, tally a little more nearly. That would really be doing good work for Luxembourg.

Marie d'Autriche, sister of Charles V, did a great deal—more, perhaps, than any one else—to strengthen the fortifications, but it was not until 1765 that the great vaults which can be seen to-day were made. These vaults, resembling catacombs, have a total length of 410 feet, and are in two parallel galleries, 11 feet wide and 10 feet high. They are provided with loopholes. Hence it gets the name the people give it—" huolen Zant," or " hollow tooth." In its war days the great rock was not unlike a modern battleship, being able to concentrate its fire in front or on either side. There was room for twenty-five batteries—twelve on the Pfaffenthal side and thirteen facing the Grund.

---

[1] " To the goddess Diana Quintus Postumius, having gained his wish, fulfils his promise."

Shortly before those excavations were made—in
1735—the Bock, which, of course, was strongly
walled all round, was connected with the town by
the massive Pont du Château, still standing and
very well preserved. It had an upper and lower
pathway, and below it ran a subterranean passage
for use should the bridge have been destroyed during
an attack.

Looking out from the southern side of the Bock,
one has an excellent view of the Rham plateau with
its ruined fortifications. Upon that height it is said
that a Roman camp existed. The plateau is made
very distinctive by four ruined towers, built by
Wenceslas II in 1393. Germans, Austrians and
Spaniards all added their quota to the military works
on the height, which, with its matchless green of
trees and turf, is extremely picturesque. Between
the Rham plateau and the Bock lies the quaint old
part of the town called Grund, packed between
heights and river. A curious place it is, with a very
interesting church. Surrounded by a maze of old
dwellings, many very seriously dilapidated, rises the
parish church of St. John. The Benedictines had it
first, after its erection in 1309 by Henry VII,
Emperor of Germany and Count of Luxembourg.
In the chapel a curious piece of sculpture is to be
seen. It is "La Ste Vierge noire" (or
" d'Egypte "), carved in wood, and remarkable for
the expression which the artist has succeeded in
imparting to the face. The Gothic baptismal fonts,
too, are noteworthy. In this church the bones of
John the Blind rested for a long time. They were

ALTAR IN THE CHAPEL OF ST. QUIRINUS, LUXEMBOURG.

To face p. 64.

interred in the crypt behind the high altar, a plaque indicating the spot. Above the crypt rose the monument which, as I have already mentioned, is to be seen in the Cathedral.

Following the river upwards, along the rue Münster and the Bisserweg, is the Bisser Gate—a most interesting walk with the Rham plateau on the left and the south-eastern extremity of the high town, upon which are situated the St. Esprit barracks, on the right—a three or four hundred yards' walk will bring the visitor to perhaps the most curious little chapel in all the world. It is situated on the right bank of the Petrusse, a little below the Viaduct and just opposite the spot where the gasworks introduce a black spot into the scene. This is the chapel of St. Quirinus (locally called Greinskapelle or Sanct Grein). Except for its frontage, the chapel is formed entirely by an excavation in the solid rock. It is the most ancient place of worship known to exist in the country, and is believed to have been hollowed out as early as the beginning of the fourth century. The façade, according to an inscription, dates from 1355. Inside, the chapel is about eight or nine yards long, six broad and five high. The altar is finely carved. No doubt sacrifices were offered up here, for a gutter leads from a rough incision in the rock to a basin. Most likely sheep were slain, as the chapel is commonly held to have been in its earliest days the place to which the primitive shepherds came to offer adoration to the deity who guarded their flocks. Outside is a pulpit carved out of the rock, and not far away is one of those miracle springs of water so numerous in Luxembourg. Even now the people believe that the water has curative powers in connection with eye diseases and scrofula. For centuries the Spring of St. Quirinus was a place of pilgrimage, and to-day when people come to the Feast of the Ste Vierge de Notre Dame, to which I have already referred, on the first of the two Sundays they go to the spring, bathe their eyes, and listen to instruction and exhortation from the outside pulpit. Not many yards away is another chapel, much smaller and more modern than that of St. Quirinus. On the exterior there is a representation of its patron, St. Wendelin, saint of the flocks, and, by some so regarded, god of the shepherds. This tiny place has a most extraordinary relic of ancient times. It is a group, carved in wood, representing three female figures, one with the eyes bandaged, sitting upon a mule. They are commonly regarded as the Christianization of either the three Hecates or the Norns, the three fates of Scandinavian mythology.

A charming walk, during which is obtained a delightful glimpse of Luxembourg, is to return to the Bisser Gate, go under the railway, and take the Trier road—that leading along the right bank of the Alzette. On reaching the powder-mill, take the twisting pathway to the left which leads up to the beautiful height, Dinselberg. On reaching the Remich road the visitor should walk along it towards the town until a path descending to Clausen is reached. Clausen is very prettily laid out. It has picturesque villas, and a fine church in Gothic style

—that of St. Cunégonde. In this faubourg once stood one of the finest palaces in the world, belonging to Count Ernest of Mansfeld, Governor of Luxembourg for nearly sixty years—from 1545 till 1604. In 1563 he built himself the magnificent palace which is no more. Glorious gardens encircled it ; beautiful terraces ran beside the river. The residence itself was most artistically built ; its interior was sumptuously rich with the most valuable art treasures. To-day but the merest traces of all this glory remain. The splendours of the palace scarcely outlived their creator. Madrid and Brussels, Trier and Metz and other places share them ; the gorgeous building fell quickly to ruin, as though such magnificence were too great to last.

In going from Clausen to Pfaffenthal, on the left, across the river towers the plateau of Altmünster, which is the prolongation of the Bock, and is cut off from it by the railway. There once stood there the famous Monastery of Münster, facing the entrance to the castle. Reared by Conrad I, about the time when our own Domesday Book was being compiled, it was that ruler's penance for an attack upon the Bishop of Trier. Later it was found to be in the way, from the strategic point of view, and it was razed to the ground about the middle of the sixteenth century. The monks found a home near at hand in Grund, but shortly afterwards returned to the plateau. In 1684 they were dispossessed again, and in Grund again found a home. The building they occupied there is now a prison.

The Pfaffenthal is a curious place. Its narrow

streets, its small riverside dwellings, its disarray of buildings are looked down upon by magnificent wooded heights, some of the natural charms of which seem to have fallen to deck here and there the Vale of the Monks. Goethe loved the picturesque spot. For a little while in 1792 he stayed at a house, still inhabited and having a plaque with these words :—

Hier wohnte Goethe
vom 14 bis 22 October
1792.

It is near the Caserne de Vauban, a building which has been reconstructed to be a temporary home for the treasures of the Archæological and Natural History Museum. "This part of the town," said Goethe, " is a veritable Elysium." The Vauban mentioned is, of course, the famous soldier Sébastien le Prestre de Vauban (1633–1707), marshal of France, and one of the most celebrated of military engineers. Part of the fortifications of Luxembourg are his work, and much that he introduced into the art of war still remains. He conducted fifty successful sieges, constructed or rebuilt a hundred and sixty fortresses, and took part in three hundred fights. " Perhaps the most honest and virtuous man of his age," Saint-Simon said of him. He foretold, eighty years in advance, the coming in force of those doctrines which caused the French Revolution. The Republicans scattered his remains, but his name lives, in Luxembourg and in history, and his heart rests in Les Invalides, placed there by that other great military genius, Napoleon Bonaparte.

Photo by (Dr. Fischer, Luxembourg.

OLD LUXEMBOURG: SUBURB OF GRUND.

To face p. 72.

GOETHE'S HOUSE, LUXEMBOURG.

The museum, containing also a library and the archives, is exceedingly interesting. The library contains no fewer than twenty thousand volumes and five or six hundred manuscripts dealing mainly with the history of the country. In the archives are forty thousand documents in which can be read the story of the great families of the land. The oldest document bears the date 803. The museum itself is particularly notable for its very fine collection of Gallo-Roman antiquities. There is a large number of remarkably beautiful vases, some of which are unique. Six thousand Roman coins and several hundred Celtic, all found in the Grand Duchy, make a striking collection. Bronzes, statuettes, ornaments, ivories and many other kinds of treasure are to be seen in large numbers. All these objets d'art are, perhaps, not seen to advantage in such a building, and it is to be hoped that before long they will have a resting-place worthy of their value and beauty. The natural history section, too, is most interesting, and botany is represented by something like sixty thousand specimens.

Clausen and the Pfaffenthal are looked down upon by three most picturesque wooded heights—the Parkhöhe, the Obergrünewald and the Niedergrünewald. They are delightful heights to wander on, especially the middle one, from which charming and ever-varying vistas of the town present themselves to the eye. At the extremity of the Obergrünewald is the old Fort Thüngen (Trois Glands or Drei Eicheln). The fort carries a sad memory for Luxembourg people, for in its ditch the prisoners taken by the

French in the Peasants' Revolt against them were shot.

Such, then, are the charms and attractions of Luxembourg, and it must be admitted that for such a little city they are strikingly numerous. It has a rich dower of everything that calls the wanderer, many

> Elusive notes in wandering wafture borne
> From undiscoverable lips that blow
> An immaterial horn.

[Dr. Tucker, Luxembourg.

ON THE OUTSKIRTS OF LUXEMBOURG.

To face p. 74.

ON BOTH SIDES OF THE
SOUTHERN BORDER

Allons! The road is before us!
It is safe—I have tried it—my own feet have tried it well . .
Camerado, I will give you my hand.

WALT WHITMAN.

CHAPTER III

ON BOTH SIDES OF THE SOUTHERN BORDER

To do southern Luxembourg something like the justice it deserves, one might paraphrase Isaac Walton's reference to a strawberry : Doubtless God could create a more beautiful country, but—of its kind—doubtless God never did. It is essentially a district for the wanderer afoot. It has not the Dantesque topography of the Echternach region or the Müllerthal, but, with northern Lorraine, it shares a simple and pleasing charm. Visitors will find it, indeed, somewhat difficult to decide to which Nature has been the kinder, so alike are those twin sisters upon whom she has showered her favours with no niggard hand. In both lands one finds the ebb and flow of a quiet human life ; they live together on the very best of terms. It is often difficult to say where exactly is the frontier line. Once, during a wander from Mondorf to Rodemack, I found that many people did not know where the border line was. Some said it was the tiny Altbach which runs round Mondorf. Others said it was not, but could add no definite information. It was really a matter of small importance to them, so long as they knew roughly where they were. Later, in seeking a spot

from which to take a photograph of the town, I came
across a plaque with the word " Landesgrenze." It
was loosely nailed to a pig-sty beside the sluggish
little brook ! Nothing could be less like a frontier
than the Altbach—no customs house, no guards, not
an ordinarily visible sign that the bridge across it
carries one from the Duchy into the mighty realm
of the Emperor William, into the " black provinces "
of the French school-map.

And as yet across that very indistinct frontier
Germanization has not penetrated very deeply. If one
wayfarer salutes you with " Guten Tag ! " the next
will most likely say " Bonjour ! " In the little wayside inns one man's " Prosit ! " will be answered by
another's " A Vous ! " And still it cannot be said
that the people of this corner of Lorraine have
become even moderately French. At heart they are
neither French nor German, but Luxembourgers,
clinging among themselves very tenaciously to the
dialect of the Duchy. The Treaty of Versailles
(1769) fixed upon the Altbach as Luxembourg's
frontier for a mile or two above and below Mondorf.
Marie Thérèse, therefore, had to surrender a strip
of Luxembourg's territory on the right bank of the
brook, territory which includes the ancient Duchy
" seigneuries " of Rodemack, Puttelange, Roussy and
Preisch. The year 1871 rather aggravated than
lessened the wrong of this piece of bad map-making.

From the west, from the sparkle and rich beauty
of the Chiers Valley—the Chiers, by the way, is the
only river of the Duchy which wanders westwards—
to the east, to the proud, vine-fringed Mosel, southern

MONDORF.

To face p. 95.

Luxembourg has a great deal wherewith to reward the stranger. Beautiful woods are scattered over all, in fawn and green and gold ; good roads lead everywhere, and the olive of every valley is threaded with the argent of a rippling stream. So highly favoured by climate, so plentifully provided with fresh water and mineral streams, the good lands of the south, extraordinarily fertile, make an El Dorado for the Nature-lover in general and the botanist in particular ; they are the home of an almost bewildering array of flowers and ferns. At two seasons of the year is the country glorious—in spring, when Nature promises, and if

> April's anger is swift to fall,
> April's wonder is worth it all,

and in autumn, season of fulfilment and victory, when the woods show every hue from red to russet, when flowers still bloom, when, with colours still bravely flying and with a rejoicing heart, the world marches to meet winter. The flowers of the south are early bloomers ; proud orchid and humble bluebell respond quickly to the call of the warm winds. Hedgerow, field and riverside vie with one another to be first in spring array. Quickly the March winds give the carpets of the woodlands their spring-cleaning, and soon " delicate windflowers dancing light " are here, there and everywhere.

> Squirrel is climbing swift and lithe,
> Chiff-chaff whetting his airy scythe,
> Woodpecker whirrs his rattling rap,
> Ringdove flies with a sudden clap.

Rook is summoning rook to build,
Dunnock his beak with moss has filled,
Robin is bowing in coat-tails brown,
Tomtit chattering upside down.

Down along the river-bed, beside "the first of
trees," [1] matching harmoniously the water's chain of
sunbeams, the beautiful rose-flowered water-plant
(*Butomus umbellatus*) very frequently finds a home.
In a sunny day's wander by hill and wood the visitor
will see on either hand cornflower and moonwort,
speedwell, medlar and anemone, foxglove, hart's
tongue and adder's tongue, hellebore and a hundred
other beauties of the countryside. With luck and
a sharp eye, he may even find, on the spreading
mossy masses on rocks and tree-stems in moist
places, that beautiful filmy fern, *Hymenophyllum tun-
bridgense,* which, though with a local and a northern
name, is the most widely distributed of its family and
more common in the southern than in the northern
hemisphere. And how rich is this little country in
orchids ! Of the twenty-four distinct kinds and the
hundred and eleven varieties known to exist in
Europe, no fewer than eighteen kinds and forty-two
varieties are to be found in Luxembourg, mostly in
the south. North and south, in short, seem to have
in southern Luxembourg a happy meeting-place.
From the north Flora sends her frailer children
and from the south her hardier to find a home in
and to beautify this part of a beautiful Duchy.

Southern Luxembourg can be "done" by rail ;
it can only be thoroughly appreciated if explored

---

[1] A Finnish description of willows.

afoot. The wanderer's best guides are the little gods of the open air. They will lead him into the soft twilight of fancy from the hard, full day of reality ; by the rivers nymphs will be his truest companions if he would hear the water's song "coming in solemn beauty like slow old tunes of Spain " ; and for the woodlands let the dryad lead the way by mossy paths with " a slow, sweet piece of music from the grey forgotten years." Or—as the reader may prefer advice in strictly modern terms —I say, in short, wander just where you will, distances are nowhere great, and if you are compelled to miss something which may be away by a road on the left, you are certain to find something to compensate for it not far along the alternative path. Give your wander-fancy the freest rein, the following being either regarded as hints or as pictures which may recall something from " the past, its ripe pleasance," when the journey is over.

I wander, then, first to the extreme south-western corner of the Duchy, leaving the capital by the Avenue Monterey. It is a delightful road ; there are little villages to salute on the way, small history-less places where every passer-by is an event. The charm of such villages as Dippach and Bascharage lies in their cafés. Curious little resorts they are, the very names of which help to carry one still farther on one's journey from the workaday world and raise the illusion of really being in another age. And when one thinks of medical and sanitary science one wonders how the people contrive to live and to be so healthy as they undoubtedly are. Some way

or other they manage to make a mockery of the
precautions which enlightened city corporations insist
on, and yet the muscle and blood are here created
which go to reinforce the weakening fibre of city
life. The children playing about are sturdy little
mites ; the men have a splendid physique ; the
women show a certain degree of handsomeness even
when age advances and are picturesque in their short
cotton skirts, bulgy blouses, strong loose boots and
straw sun-hats. In the tiny cafés they become
talkative, adding to one's knowledge in a speech
which might be musical with care, but in which
they appear to emphasize the harsh notes. To a
visitor the wayside café takes the place of guide-
book and newspaper. He may have the latest news
there in the rare event of anything having happened ; he may have folklore or the history of any
person or place within a wide range ; he will mostly
find a guide should he require one. When in doubt
place your troubles before the old dame who pre-
sides over the nearest café. And the names of those
little cafés, and the streets and " places " of the
villages, show the simple faith of those simple people.
To them there is a great deal in a name. That a
small inn should be called " Au Bon Dieu " was
a real relief to the traveller and the village people
of old. The villages give outward evidence of their
faith by calling one ruelle " la rue des Trois Saints,"
and a shapeless little " place " " la Place de la
Sainte Vierge." Names everywhere are in keeping
with the old-world atmosphere created by the odd-
looking houses, now of stone, now of wood, now of

both. And an evening in any one of those wayside villages, made up as a rule of a cluster of houses at cross-roads, will teach the wanderer more about a people than any " personally conducted tour " ever planned.

A little beyond Bascharage the sinuous Chiers is reached, and across it lies the Black Country of Luxembourg, thoughtfully stowed away by Nature in a corner of the land. To get a good view of this district the best plan is to climb from Rodange ¹ up to the bastion-like summit of Titelberg. This rugged plateau was the site of a Roman camp, and bits of the guard-house are discovered even to-day. The name is said to be derived from Titusberg, and that from Titus Labienus, the Roman warrior about whose doings in the neighbourhood the meagre history which exists is wildly contradictory. The time to reach the summit is just before the sunrise, when the gorgeous rose of dawn, heralding a summer's day, flushes all the east. Then the beauties of the wide landscape are opened up to the sight like those of a Jericho rose. In a wide, irregular semicircle the Chiers runs round from east to west ; the green uplands of neighbouring France and Belgium catch the glories of renascent day, till all around glows in the full glory of the light. Then the rings and rows of furnaces, the black patches of iron ore and refuse, are clearly seen. Yet one does not resent those " warts " ; they are riches in black.

¹ The suffix -ange, in France -igne, -ignes, -igny, -igney, in Germany -ingen, in England -ing, found with a family name, signifies a family settlement.

Round Rodange, Differdange and Esch-sur-Alzette six thousand workmen bring to the surface nearly seven million tons of iron ore per annum. Luxembourg's Black Country is not large but it is exceedingly rich, and one cannot grudge to industry one part of a country where Nature has so much of its own way. At evening, too, the view from Titelberg is enchanting, when the silvery grey of twilight makes a garment which even the furnace smoke does not barbarously stain with its carbon strokes. At nightfall the scene has a new charm. That is the Cinderella-hour, when the light goes and leaves her golden slipper, the Star of Eve, in the stairway of the sky. To come down from Titelberg, skirt the Grand Bois which lies along the little piece of frontier which France throws up against the Duchy ; to cross the fields and take the woodland way to where Differdange lies in its circle of mines, is one of the most interesting and pleasant walks in the southern country.

Differdange, a fine large industrial village, can be made the headquarters for some interesting excursions. Eastwards and on the way to Belvaux lie two peaks—Soleuvre, the higher (its other name is Zolwerknapp), and Lestchef. On the former was a Roman camp—the reader will note that south Luxembourg has a chain of such forts—which eventually gave place to the inevitable castle from which the lords of Soleuvre exercised wide sway from the eleventh until nearly the end of the sixteenth century, when the fortress was, during the reign of Henry III, taken by the French, destroyed, and never rebuilt.

Some remains of both camp and castle are still to be seen on the height, which is, by the way, one of the highest in Luxembourg. After the destruction of the castle, the ejected seigneurs came to Differdange to live, and the castle, still standing in ruins there, was their abode. Part of a monastery, built by the Cistercian order in the fourteenth century, is pointed out—an ordinary dwelling-house.

Belvaux has a delightful situation. On the left is the Côte de Belvaux, where the Chiers has its rise, and not far away in the opposite direction is the Bel-Val source, whence comes that excellent mineral water so often seen on Grand Duchy tables. The water springs from a fault in jurassic rock and maintains an even temperature of 10° C. Since 1893 the spring has been yielding not less than 12,500 litres per hour. And now Esch-sur-Alzette—there is another Esch, on the Sure—is not far away. With its seventeen or eighteen thousand inhabitants, it is the second largest town in the Duchy. It has had a curious history. Being a border town, it was constantly plundered and set on fire during the warlike times of old, and gradually sank to the status of a very small village. Peace made it grow a little again, but only a quarter of a century ago it had little more than a thousand inhabitants. Industry has made it prosperous, and it is certainly the newest town in the country. There are two large ironworks and numerous small concerns. Amongst the people one hears the Luxembourg patois, French, German and Italian all mixed up in, to the visitor, most hopeless fashion. No remnants of the old fortifications remain, though they were formidable in their day, and on the site of the old castle of Berward an industrial magnate has reared ironworks which, in the people's description, is still " le château." The most pleasant way to reach Bettembourg is by way of Kâyl, on the Kâylbach, a pretty stream running through woodlands from Lorraine, and joining the Alzette at Noertzange, a mile or two to the north. Beside Kâyl stands Mont Saint Jean, roughly 1,500 feet high. On the summit was, of course, a castle in the castle days, which the French destroyed at the same time as they sacked that on Soleuvre. Where the castle stood there is now a humble chapel. This is dedicated to John the Baptist, and is, on the Sunday following the 24th of June, the place of an annual pilgrimage and a yearly fair, similar to that of Helperknapp.[1]   A magnificent view is obtained from the chapel. The peaks of the High Ardennes round Arlon and Longwy can easily be distinguished ; the winding Kâylbach and Alzette can be traced along their lovely valleys, with the olive mass of the Forest of Bettembourg as a background. On particularly sunny days, so it is said, the high towers of Luxembourg send heliograph flashes from afar. When the weather is clear, Mont Saint Jean can be seen when one stands beside the St. Esprit Barracks at Luxembourg. The distance is thirteen kilometres as the crow flies, and sometimes the range of vision includes Mont de Soleuvre, two or three kilometres farther off. Wander down into the little village of Dudelange ; seek the inn and ask for food and

[1] See pp. 306–7.

drink ; chat with any old Dudelange-ite whom you chance to meet, and you will hear a story of French Revolution times. Empires may fall and emperors die, the modern world may be convulsed, but there is one constantly repeated story which Dudelange likes to dwell on better than anything up-to-date, however stirring. If it should happen to be May 17th you may hear Mass for the souls of some long dead. And this is the story. Dudelange in 1794 was a little village of seventy or eighty inhabitants, and the tiny place was much disturbed by the ravages of the vicious soldiers of the Republic of Reason. The people of the village joined with those of Esch and Kâyl to defend their territory, and on several occasions repulsed the French troops. The heroic defenders of the village, however, had to give way in the end before force of numbers, and in revenge the French troops sacked and burned Dudelange, massacring nearly all the inhabitants of the village, sparing neither age nor youth, compelling some to dig their graves before execution. The massacre accounted for some sixty or seventy persons, and it is for the repose of their souls that Mass is sung to-day. Seldom has wrong penetrated so deeply into the soul of a little community. For that Dudelange has always associated the French with all that is most evil. The memory of that butchery and its losses is one which nothing that France could ever do could possibly wipe out. To-day the ill-will finds fiery expression as though the deed were of yesterday's doing.

From Dudelange a pleasant walk brings the

wanderer to the quiet little village of Bettembourg, where he has left well behind the Black Country of Luxembourg. In that tranquil spot there is a large and finely organized retreat for the aged, and a visit to it will show how admirably the Duchy deals with her broken soldiers from all ranks of life.

And on the tramp northwards along the glorious valley of the Alzette one leaves behind the gently sloping country which spreads from Lorraine into Luxembourg, and when the wide valley ends at Fentange a different landscape comes before the wanderer, who, with Rosalind, will exclaim : "Well, here is the forest of Arden!" Fentange church, by the way, is worth visiting to see the fine picture of "Luther at the Diet of Augsburg."

Mondorf is a miniature Matlock : it may one day be a wealthy Wiesbaden. An irregular little town, by merit of its curative waters "raised to that Bad eminence" which it enjoys, it is very humble. Its claims to recognition are not heralded by means of four-colour posters in the great railway stations ; I doubt if Harley Street knows it well enough to prescribe it to those who have lived Society's season too well. Mondorf may have herself to blame. She has not worried to lay out her streets ; they have just happened ; they are the more or less well-paved spaces which inevitably occur between rows of houses. True, she has a park, prettily designed with lake and kiosk and an up-to-date établissement des bains. But Mondorf has not yet decided to be fashionable. Her chief street is the "Mühlenweg" instead of

Photo by]   [F. Scharff-Vandèr, Luxembourg.

HESPERANGE.

the "Grand Boulevard"; the best name she has achieved for an hotel, after exhausting all the banalities like Hôtel des Bains and Hôtel de la Gare, is Hôtel du Grand-Chef, which does not suggest that Spartan humbleness of diet which invalids would like friends at home to associate with a stay at a "ville balnéaire." The jaded Parisian and Parisienne, the worn Londoner, must really be properly considered, and Mondorf should remember that the Biblical leper was not the last person to object to having to bathe in an out-of-the-way place when there are others of more resounding names and with more fashionable inducements.

The prospect of the company of a hotelful of persons all more or less invalids should not deter the wanderer in Luxembourg from visiting the little Kurort. The walk from Luxembourg is only twelve miles through interesting and delightful country. South-east from the city the road, tree-shaded, leads, carrying one, some time before Hesperange is reached, to a great, bare plateau high above a deep, wooded gorge of the Alzette, which suddenly, with its surroundings, bursts radiantly and surprisingly upon the view. A sloping mile brings one to the little town of Hesperange, lying snugly on both banks of the Alzette and framed by gently rising hills. From its midst rise the ruins, still at places over a hundred feet high, of the ancient castle, once the hereditary domain of the lords of Rodemack. The crumbling walls are singularly picturesque and noble, but some stormy night I should imagine the highest remaining will come crashing down upon the houses, built of the castle stones, which nestle so closely by the remnant of the old bourg. The lords of Rodemack were long famous for their heart-whole support of the kings of France against the House of Burgundy. They eventually roused the anger of the Emperor Maximilian, who vowed war without mercy. He laid siege to Hesperange Castle (in 1483), took it, razed it to the ground, and confiscated the domains of his enemies. In ruins, the fine castle, bearing traces which carry back its story to the ninth century, has remained to this day, yet another desolate, dusty relic of an order of things long passed away.

The traveller should turn aside to visit the little coquettish village of Itzig, or he may reach Hesperange by way of it. It dates from Roman times, and here, too, once stood an altar to Neptune. The most interesting thing to be seen, however, is the original agreement, preserved in the church, for the capitulation of the fortress of Luxembourg on June 10, 1795, to the forces of the French Republic after its seven months' siege.

At Hesperange the Alzette leaves the long, wide, and beautiful Roeser Valley. Here the banks of the river are low, and every winter the water, Nile-like, floods and fertilizes the surrounding lands. Nowhere else in the Duchy is agricultural land so valuable ; it costs two or three hundred pounds an acre. One may either keep on the main road to Mondorf or take that which leads up the valley, a glorious walk, going as far as Roeser and then cutting across country almost due east to Mondorf. This district is made extremely interesting by a large number of coquettish little villages—Weiler-la-Tour (the Roman Turris Villaris), keeping only its name out of the past ; Aspelt, dating from 963, and preserving the remains of the feudal manor, the castle of a family strong at the time of Henry IV and John the Blind ; Altwies, a little garden village where every open space grows its roses ; Dalheim, with its fine Roman camp. And so to Mondorf by any one of a variety of ways—all lined with apple-trees. These long miles of apple avenues are a constant delight to the wanderer, and it is curious to notice the artistry of their arrangement. Sometimes white and rosy-cheeked apple-trees alternate for miles ; sometimes it is red, russet and white for kilometre after kilometre. Yet the people would not agree with the poet who, singing of the goddesses, says :—

> Pomona, provider of tanged autumn cider,
> Our lady of apples, she's easily first !

No, in a country of apple-trees and vines, these hardy people are mostly beer-drinkers.

That mineral water which has given Mondorf some degree of fame, a slight taste of celebrity, was accidentally discovered a little more than half a century ago when engineers were boring in the hope of finding a salt spring. The boring was continued to a depth of nearly 2,500 feet, and was at that time the deepest artesian well in Europe. The waters were first privately exploited, but in 1886 were taken over by the State. The supply amounts to 36,360 litres (slightly over 8,000 gallons) an hour. The water is similar to that of Homburg, Kissingen and

Wiesbaden. I cannot enter into medical and scientific details, but I have been given to understand on high authority that the water is vastly superior to that of those places mentioned. For the benefit of those whom it may concern, no doubt, an authoritative statement in which that declaration is made hastens to declare that "Mondorf has not, like many other 'stations balnéaires,' the enervating excitements of a 'grande ville.' The Luxembourg resort only desires to attract those who are ill and wish to become well, not those who are well with the intention of making them ill." And the list of ailments that eau de Mondorf can cure is formidable ; it will make you grow and make you eat ; it stretches the octave in cures. On the outskirts of the town is the large establishment of the Sisters of St. Elizabeth, who receive invalids requiring special care.

Mondorf is certainly, even at the height of the season, a quiet, restful little place. If the water is excellent, the air is no less so. The park in which the établissement thermal stands is quite close to the town, and part of the grounds are really in Lorraine territory. The principal building is a beautiful rustic erection. On the rez-de-chaussée are the bathing cabinets as well as those for the different treatments provided. Above is a handsome reading-room (often used in the evening for dancing), a ladies' room, a billiard saloon, a café and a roomy terrace. Two other buildings contain large swimming-baths. All the latest medical appliances are in use, and the whole establishment is of the most up-to-date character. The park, too, is charmingly laid out, and has an area of about forty acres. The flower-beds are glorious throughout the long summer, and the entire park with its lovely alleys is shaded with fine trees. On the Altbach, which skirts it, canoes and rowing-boats are numerous ; cascades murmur here and there ; there is good fishing. During the season, from the beginning of May till the beginning of October, three concerts are given daily in the park, and at the casino two dances weekly. A great covered promenade makes exercise possible during rainy days, which are, however, few and far between.

But even if the fact that Mondorf is a Vichy of the north be no attraction to the wanderer, there is this much to be said in favour of a stay in this most restful little village. It is a fine centre for walking or cycling tours in the interesting district in which it stands. Seeing that the frontier is so easily crossed, the visitor to Luxembourg's sunny south should certainly pay a visit to Rodemack. That means but an afternoon's tramp through historical and beautiful country. Of all old places in this district none has so well preserved its ancient state as has the old fortress and seigneurie capital, Rodemack. It is reached in about an hour by taking the Thionville road for a little while and then turning off to the right. The first village to be reached is Puttelange, which as far back as 907 had achieved the dignity of "city." Archbishops of Trèves were delighted to honour the place, and from about the middle of the thirteenth century until the French

Revolution it and its parish, which included seven neighbouring villages, were under the beneficent sway of the famous Abbey of Echternach. The Benedictines from there, too, built its fine church, which is notable for a remarkable painting on the walls of the choir. The work of a lay friar of the abbey, it reproduces something of the artistic effect of the frescoes in the Church of St. Paulin at Trèves and represents the baptism of Clovis, together with a number of legendary incidents connected with the lives of the three myrtr-saints Firmin, Quirinus and Féréole. That saintly trio enjoyed great veneration in this district, and at Puttelange especially they were invoked to cure disease. At the foot of the ruelle leading up to the church is a beautiful cross in stone in their honour. It is stated to have been erected in about the middle of the eighteenth century, but there are doubts upon that point, some authorities holding that it was only restored then, as the base of the monument—a representation of Christ's tomb—is certainly sixteenth-century work. A little farther on, and a few yards to the right along the road leading to Himlingen, stands an ancient " croix de franchise." Here in old times justice was administered, civil actions decided and local ceremonies performed. The cross has been standing since 1643, and is one of the very few of its kind not thrown down at the time of the Revolution. About that time, too, was built the Castle of Puttelange, which is to be seen a little farther along the road. That manor replaced the old feudal building pillaged and burned by the Swedes in 1636.

THE GATE OF RODEMACK.

To face p. 95

The road, girt by apple-trees all the way, passes through a pretty wood, on leaving which a tiny roadside chapel is seen on the left. Then the way leads down for a few hundred yards to where Rodemack, fronted by great chestnut-trees, stands.

Rodemack is undoubtedly one of the most curious villages in the whole of the Grand Duchy. It still stands huddled within the walls from behind which it saw so much border fighting. One enters it to-day by the same gate, marvellously preserved—though the Administration des Postes might have avoided fixing telegraph wires to one of its towers !—by which Henry II, King of France, entered the town in 1552. The streets are narrow and twisting, the houses old, and not one of them possesses a garden, the only garden in the place being attached to the manor house in the middle of the little town., I visited the place on a Sunday afternoon, a time when the inhabitants appear to indulge in siestas, for it was outwardly deserted from end to end, giving one, perhaps, a better impression of its age than it would otherwise have done. It seemed to have come bodily out of the Middle Ages ; if knights of old in shining armour had come riding through the gateway their appearance would have been the most natural thing in the world, so mediæval was the scene. But the illusion was spoiled ; a motor-car snorted, came cautiously through the narrow portal, and the chauffeur disturbed the afternoon repose of mine host of the " Golden Lion " by loud demands for—petrol. So I went into the church, which dates from 1783. Here is to be seen the mausoleum of one of the proudest of Rodemack's seigneurs—" Herman-Fortunat, Margrave of Baden and of Hochberg, Lord of Rodemack," who was buried there in 1665, the sepulchre being opened two years later to receive the body of his wife—" Marie-Sidonie, née de Daun, Countess of Falkenstein, Lady of Limbourg, of Rodemack, etc." Several other members of the family are interred in the church.

The lords of Rodemack were perhaps the most powerful feudal people of their day. At times they governed all Luxembourg ; at times their sway was acknowledged not a foot beyond their fortress walls. Their power ebbed and flowed in fickle fashion. Of those who ruled the Duchy the most famous was Gilles IV, who, at the time of John the Blind, boasted that he had the largest castle in the Duchy. And the boast was true. He handed down to his successor not only this great castle but a string of forts, including Hesperange, Useldange, Richemont, Boulay, Forbach, Neuerbourg and Cronenbourg—one of the wealthiest domains of the age. But wealth bred ambition, and constant " little wars " sapped the strength of the lords and their broad lands. At last things became so desperate that Gerard de Rodemack, last of his line, in 1483, in company with his nephew, the Count of Wirnebourg, resolved on a desperate gamble. They picked a quarrel with the Emperor, and set out with their retainers to devastate the country up to the walls of Luxembourg. The Imperial forces, however, swept them backwards, laid siege to their stronghold, and took it. The Rodemack domains were confiscated, and the Emperor gave them to the then Governor of Luxembourg, Christopher, Margrave of Baden, not so much because this particular nobleman was a favourite but because the Emperor was very deeply in his debt for ready cash. Until the time of the Revolution the castles and lands remained in that family's hands, and were finally ceded to France, when the Margrave Charles Frederick left his feudal seat and a small French garrison marched in. Rodemack gave Napoleon one of his field-marshals—Field-Marshal Simmer (a common name still in the town), whom Bonaparte made a baron on the field of Wagram. Simmer was the son of a small tradesman ; his name will be seen on the Arc de Triomphe as one of the heroes of La Grande Armée.

The castle itself is extremely interesting. A stiff climb leads up to it, and one can see that, under ancient conditions of strategy, it was a formidable place. The ancient walls, though renovated at various times, are preserved in such a manner as to give an excellent idea of the fortress which, with the exception of the capital of the Duchy, saw more war than any other. About forty years ago the castle was acquired by the Baron de Gargan, a wealthy Lorraine landed proprietor, who has done a great deal to preserve it. In a modern building, which serves as the officers' quarters, the Baron has brought together a very fine collection of objets d'art and antiquities. There are many pictures of the Flemish school, specimens of eighteenth-century stained glass, arms, furniture, porcelain, tapestry and books— making a most admirable and interesting museum.

7

The fortress, too, has great vaults and deep wells, and from its walls one looks over a wide expanse of Lorraine. Flowers and vines have been planted where once grim walls stood and cannon were ranged. Rodemack has been declared a national monument, and must, therefore, be preserved by the community as it is.

The little town's war record is striking. Some of the famous figures of history who have led forces against it are Robert de la Mark (1514), a Duke of Orleans (1543), a Duke of Guise (1558), Marshal de Créquy (1667) and a Prince of Brunswick (1792). The Government of France sold the domain in 1811, but re-bought it in 1815. General Hugo (father of the poet and then Governor of Thionville) sent the Count de Varda with about four hundred men and a couple of cannon to occupy it, and ten days after the battle of Waterloo this tiny force was attacked by ten thousand Prussians with ten cannon. The attack lasted for three days, and owing to the energetic way in which the defence was carried on the Prussians, thinking that the town was held by a very considerable force, withdrew, having lost about three hundred men.

In this corner of the Duchy there are many Roman remains, and at Dalheim was one of the long line of camps by means of which the Cæsars held the country of the Trèvirians. In addition, the wedge of high land, sloping gently from the middle towards the two rivers and running into the angle made by Mosel and Altbach, is among the most beautiful

parts of the whole Duchy. Indeed, there is scarcely
a more charming view than that which the wanderer
obtains when he climbs up the road between Mondorf
and Remich to see from the height of land the wide,
silvery Mosel gleaming beyond a countryside thickly
covered with woods and vineyards, a gorgeous spread
of green.

Before descending to the Mosel Valley, however,
the visitor should see the Roman camp at Dalheim,
the Pompeii of the Grand Duchy, which is only three
miles due north of Mondorf. The camp is to be
found on a high plateau beside the pretty little
village, and from it one may trace one's way back
to Titelberg and the Mont de Soleuvre till the eyes'
way is barred by the smoke of the Black Country,
though gleaming through the thinner fringe of grey
on the left will be seen, through the gap of the
Mosel Valley, the dim silhouette of the superb
cathedral of Metz. The Dalheim camp was the most
important military station between Titelberg and
Alttrier, and was connected by road with both these
places as well as with Trèves, Arlon and Metz.
The remains of the camp show that its shape was
oblong. To-day bushes and flowering shrubs grow
all round it, and in the centre rises a rather clumsy
obelisk, on which is a gilded ball carrying a Roman
eagle with outstretched wings. The monument, a
landmark for miles round, was erected in 1855 by
the Government from some of the débris of the
camp. The inscriptions placed upon it might well
have been simplified, such a lot of time can be
spent over them. Two are in Latin, one in French

and one in German. That in French is the masterpiece. It states :—

>   Rome a campé sur ce plateau.

And nothing could exceed the simplicity and completeness of that. It says all that need be said. But
we are informed in Latin of the circumstances of
the erection of the monument and of the generosity
of the State. The third, an eye-worrying mixture
of capital and minuscule, is an expression of rejoicing that Mars has retreated before Ceres.
Curiously enough, however, while rejoicing at the
going of Mars, the monument is clearly to the god
of war. But Peace has hers in the radiant country-
side. The remaining inscription is in German, and
says :—

>   Zeugend entstieg ich den drei Trümmern
>   Die hier Roms Lager zürückliess,

being a reference to Titelberg and Alttrier as well.
French wins undoubtedly, for all that is required
to bring back the legions is " Rome a campé sur
ce plateau "—and a little imagination. Three Roman
roads, running from Dalheim, can be easily traced
to-day ; they run north, south and west. Tiles,
pottery and coins have been dug up in great quantities, especially the latter. In 1852 a peasant who
was ploughing unearthed three large earthenware
vases, in which were found twenty-five thousand
Roman coins of the various Emperors up to the
reign of Constantine.

Returning to the main road, which passes near Dalheim, a five-mile tramp brings the wanderer, through ideally green country, to Bous, a fairly large village in a circle of hills. Here a relic of Rome of a different kind may be inspected. It is a fine mosaic in two parts, each about seven metres long and five wide. It is exquisite work, discovered, quite accidentally, in 1879. A farmer was engaged in the work of removing the ruins of an old house when he came across it, and in 1881 the Government erected the present hall which covers it. In this hall are also numerous Roman " finds."

Again the general aspect of the scene changes when the traveller looks across the vineyards towards the Mosel. Colour and line are different. South Luxembourg offered all colours to the eye. In the Mosel Valley green predominates. The gentle slope carries one down to a busier life than has been seen since leaving Esch. In the distance the hills overlooking the river Saar make a semicircle, deep purple with distance. Old Remich, first and last town in the Grand Duchy to see the Romans, lies by the river, in feature and pose strikingly pictur-esque. August, of all seasons in this region, is a delight. The roadside trees are yielding their basket-fuls of fruit, the vineyards are giving their harvests to make " Mosel." The days are long and sunny and the air gloriously fresh. And

> It's only August now and then.
> Ah, take the wanderer's way once more,
> 'Neath other skies, 'mid stranger men !

DOWN THE MOSEL TO
ECHTERNACH

Une terre aimée du ciel et favorisée des dieux.

Ausone.

What sign of those that fought and died
At shift of sword and sword?
The barrow and the camp abide,
The sunlight and the sward.

Kipling.

CHAPTER IV

DOWN THE MOSEL TO ECHTERNACH

THE height of land between Mondorf and Remich cuts the south-eastern corner of the Grand Duchy in two. And one can stand at no other point in Luxembourg and see the scene change so suddenly. Round Mondorf are quiet woods and patient fields, a landscape of northern tranquillity. On the eastern slope, however, Nature casts aside such raiment and dons all the charms which make the finery of Normandy. From a dozen heights, and far as the eye can reach, the green of vines and the olive and many-coloured golds of trees stretch down to the lovely Mosel, which, in silvery sweeps, flows through an immense green plain. Riverwards, through woods and vineyards, the wanderer descends to Remich, through a delightful land where Nature's touch has been the most tender. That gentle hand needed to care for the vine has given the neighbourhood the slenderest trees and the most delicate flowers ; there is patient moss for carpet ; wistful frond and exquisite turf complete the beauty on either hand, while the air has in it the whole sublime, subtle essence of summer.

For miles and miles northwards the vine and the Mosel keep company ; and as the river grows

larger, the soil becomes more fertile and the wine
finer. Remich gives only a " petit vin," but Grevenmacher, ten miles away, sends us " Moselblümchen."
At Remich, then, we stand on the outskirts of a
great vineyard, an extensive green land where spring,
summer and autumn are one gorgeous season. Little
Remich itself might be a small town cut out of
Normandy from the region of Le Petit Andely and
Gisors ; one almost looks to see a Falaise Castle
on yonder wooded height ; from the ramparts of
Domfront Castle one would see the same profound
green stillness as is here by the Mosel. The streets
of the town, twisted, narrow, steep, recall now
Beaumont le Roger, now Lisieux, now Coutances.
There is a quiet life in the place which tells little
or nothing of the storms through which it has passed.
Indeed, no town in the whole of Luxembourg has
got rid of the scars of war so easily. Remich sounds
and undoubtedly was Roman. As Remacum it knew
" the legions' iron tramp," but it faced the wrong
way. Its position, on a slope looking towards the
rising sun, was useless as a site for a camp, so the
legions climbed up the Scheuerberg and built their
wide semicircle of camps facing northwards over
the Forest of Arduenna, whence might come, and
did come, the foes of Imperial Rome. If Remich
did not serve the Romans for purposes of war, it
undoubtedly was one of their pleasure resorts.

Later in history, however, the position changed.
When Luxembourg was beginning to take something
like definite shape, Remich found itself a border town,
facing hostile lands. In the Middle Ages it was,

REMICH FROM THE MOSEL

To face p. 129.

without doubt, very strongly fortified, and for long centuries it suffered all the misfortunes of border towns in all lands in warlike times. In 882 the Normans came into the district. Having sacked and burned Trier (Trèves), they set out to take Metz. On the vast plain lying on the other side of the river from Remich they were met by hastily raised local forces, under the Bishops of Metz and Trier and Godefroid d'Ardenne. A desperate battle lasted all day, and at nightfall the local army was shattered by sheer weight of numbers. Many thousands of dead were left upon the field, including the Bishop of Metz. But, though victorious, the Normans had suffered so very heavily that they were unable to continue their march. So, having sacked and burned Remich, they retreated whence they came. During the disturbed sixteenth, seventeenth and eighteenth centuries the little town often felt all the weight of the march of hostile armies across it, but if then, fortress-decked, it looked as warlike as any other town in the Grand Duchy, to-day it has almost completely lost the savage beauty Bellona gave it. Save on the north side of the town, where an old gate leading to the quay has stood the test of time, no remnant of the once formidable and frowning fortifications is to be seen. Time has carried away everything of the age of war, and to-day Remich, a town of nearly three thousand people, presents a pretty picture of peace.

In spite of all her relics of war, in spite of so many of them having been banished, the iron of a hard past has entered the soul of the peasantry of this little land. There is a certain tristesse in their making, and in such peaceful places as Remich this innate sadness seems most noticeable. " Old, un-happy, far-off things " still appear to be held tenaciously in memory, and the Luxembourger mistrusts the future just a little. Were it not for a beautiful climate and a lovely country, what a " dour " people the Luxembourgers would be ! They would have all the resignation and monotone of the Finns. As it is, climate and scenery enliven them to some extent, but these are not sufficient to chase away a sort of brooding solemnity and aloofness, that coldness bred in the race by centuries of oppression. But if this reserve is somewhat difficult to penetrate in the Luxembourg peasant, it is far, however, from shutting him off from the visitor who wishes to make his acquaintance. Mere curiosity will seldom do it, but genuine interest will.

Remich spreads itself in an amphitheatre on the left bank of the river. Seen from the German side —a bridge, opened in 1866, connects the two banks, and the toll is a halfpenny—the town presents a long row of white and yellow houses, roofed with red tiles and blue slates, a beautiful façade, above which rises the church, with its very ancient tower. To appreciate the beauty of its surroundings, perhaps the best thing to do is to go and have lunch in the roomy, vine-covered jardin-terrasse of the Hôtel Belle Vue, Im Bourenweg. Im Bourenweg is the curious street which runs along the top of the ridge on, which the town stands, so that the veranda of the little hotel looks down the slope and up and down a long stretch of the magnificent Mosel. Besides the vine, fruit-trees are everywhere. Round Remich, indeed, is one vast garden.

No visitor should leave Remich to continue his wanderings in the Grand Duchy without paying a visit to Prussian Nennig, on the other side of the river, where the finest Roman mosaic ever discovered is to be seen. It is but a couple of miles away, along a pleasant road girt by apple, pear and chestnut trees. There is quite a number of old châteaux here and there, and every few hundred yards one comes across tiny chapels and crosses in wood and stone, some of them finely carved and evidently very old.

It was in 1852 that Nennig had fame thrust upon it by the discovery of a Roman villa with an extraordinarily beautiful mosaic. Prior to that date numerous Roman " finds "—small mosaics, coins, vases, etc.—were reported, but that of 1852 put them all in the shade. In the autumn of that year a small-holder, Pierre Reuter by name, was digging a potato-pit. His work was almost finished, when his spade struck, several times, a hard object, the contact giving out a hollow sound. He cleared away some of the soil, and a " parterre " of mosaic became visible. However, Reuter buried his potatoes in the pit, deciding that he would continue his investigations in the following year. He communicated with the archæological authorities, and these took in hand the work of clearing away the covering of earth about the mosaic, the excavation of the remains and the whole Roman villa, the erection of a hall over the mosaic, and that picturesque arrangement of everything which greets the visitor to-day. The mosaic is conspicuous in the first place for its great size. It measures fifty by thirty-three feet, and the only mosaic which exceeds such dimensions is that of Latereau. That, however, has not the great beauty of the Nennig treasure. The charm of the whole design is really magnificent ; there is nothing the least harsh about the colours ; the symmetry and execution are perfect. In the mosaic there are eight " medallions," seven of which depict the different kinds of combat of which Roman games were composed. The eighth, which is that farthest from the entrance, carries the following inscription :—

Dieser
Roemische
Mosaikfussboden
Wurde 1852 Aufgefun-
Den und 1874 unter
Wilhelm
Deutschem Kaiser und
König von Preussen
Wieder Herge-
stellt.

It is not known whether that " medallion " formerly contained a tableau, like the others, or an inscription of the time of the builder of the villa. It was just about this spot that the farmer's spade first hit the mosaic, and no doubt some damage was done. The hollow sound is accounted for by the fact that beside this plaque a basin is sunk in the floor, and below the mosaic there was a passage for the water to pass through.

Standing by this basin, and looking towards the entrance, the picture on the left represents a tiger, with a particularly savage look, in the act of dispatching a wild ass. The tableau opposite shows the lion and the slave. The man is conducting the animal to its cage after it has evidently devoured a horse, judging by all that remains, the head. These two tableaux represent the first part of the Roman games—fights between animals. Then begins the second part—combats between men and animals. In the centre of the mosaic is a tableau representing a struggle between three men and a bear. The bear has thrown one to the ground, and the two others are engaged in endeavouring to draw the animal off by means of blows from whips. The next picture, on the right of a row of three, shows the panther and the javelin-thrower. The animal has been badly wounded and is endeavouring to get rid of the lance which pierces its shoulder. The gladiator is seen with another lance, raised ready to give the coup de grâce. The two tableaux in line with this one depict the third section of the Roman games—combats between men—and the last shows a musician playing upon an organ. Beside him stands another with a great curved trumpet. One of the most striking features of the mosaic is the sixfold repetition of a large square, in the centre of which is a beautifully designed rose.

From what remains of it to-day, it is evident that the villa was one of considerable size, and the different apartments can still be traced. In the centre of the villa stood a handsome atrium, 50 feet by 30 feet, where the noble Roman who possessed the villa received his friends and banqueted them in summer-time. In front of it was a spacious terrace with, no doubt, a carefully tended garden in front. Rooms, corridors, windows, courts, baths there were, numerous and on a large scale, and the villa was certain to be artistically decorated in every way. And who was the noble Roman who, far from the revels and anxieties of Rome, some distance from that city of Roman pomp farther down the Mosel, Trier, enjoyed quiet days in this delightful spot? That is a secret which has not been wrested from the silent past. Coins of Nero and of some of his predecessors have been unearthed, but the style of the building, the fine workmanship of the mosaic, suggest a much earlier period than that. Some authorities believe that the villa was built in the reign of Hadrian, who loved peace and encouraged art. He beautified not only Rome but places far from the capital ; he had a weakness for country houses. Into the Roman art of that time Grecian influences had crept, and the experts see in the remains of the villa evidences of that particular influence. Hadrian, it is held, set an example by the style of his villas, and the builder of that at Nennig followed it.

There is another point of doubt. When the Goths and Huns engulfed the glory and the sordidness that was Rome, did they destroy the villa? Perhaps in the dust of that tremendous overthrow the villa at

Nennig was submerged too, but some say that it was still standing and in use when the Normans were marching from Trier to Metz. On the battlefield overlooked by the villa the Normans, though victorious, were, as has been related, stopped on their march, and besides sacking and burning Remich they plundered the villa and set it on fire. It was burned down ; but few stones stood on the tops of others. Gradually Mother Earth threw her protecting cover over it. Nearly a thousand times did seedtime and harvest come and go above it, until chance sent a spade deeper than usual and the villa's peerless art treasure was uncovered to delight the eye once more.

Years ago I ascended the Mosel Valley from Trier to Remich in the springtime ; last year I went the same journey in autumn. But I really cannot decide in which season I think the region is the prettier. I object to giving my vote in favour of one sort of weather against another. When a-wandering I can say, with Longfellow, " How beautiful is rain ! " and wind, even though it may

> Clothe me with fine
> Mist from the hill,

is one of the best of talkative companions, to which no poet and only one or two painters have done real justice. All weathers have something to recommend them ; in them all the world is still " a world of hidden dimples," if only the wanderer will look with seeing eyes. So when the first faint flutes of spring are sounding, or when autumn has fanned the furnace of colour, when the air is embalmed with the perfume of new-mown hay, and the gentle breezes throw around " the scent of alien meadows far away," in both seasons the wide green valley is a wanderer's paradise from the first fine thrill of dawn thrown through the prisms of the Orient to lie gloriously upon the patterned silk of vineyards, till blue-lidded eve beams softly over all. But there was something to mar last autumn's pleasure—an element of tragedy in the Mosel Valley. There had not been a great deal of sun during the summer, and the grapes did not ripen. Disease, too, had spread badly in the vineyards.

" I have never seen such a bad year for the vine," said the owner of a vineyard which I visited. " 'Mosel 1912 ' will most likely be fair vinegar, but scarcely good wine. And if the blight spreads it will strip those hillsides clear of the vine." Luckily the apple crop was almost a record one, and he showed me a tree from which he had just taken seventy-seven francs' worth of apples.

An excellent road runs along the Luxembourg side of the river, the railway hugging the Prussian strand. It is a lovely road, with slopes of green on either hand, with the river now flowing so peacefully, now breaking into cascades of silver and of melody. Then the glorious green will form the frame for a pretty little village—Stadtbredimus, Palzen, Greiweldange, Wehr, Ehnen, Wormeldange, Wincheringen, Rehlingen, Ahn, Machtum, Nittel and Wellen. Such is the sum total of them before

Grevenmacher is reached. Occasionally, too, the ruins of an ancient castle, as at Thorn and Stadt-bredimus, add to the interest and picturesqueness of the landscape. Especially is that of Thorn, on the Prussian side of the river, remarkable. It is a grey old relic with huge towers—yet another striking evidence of that powerful individualism crushed by the triumph of the community, another monument to those proud lords who are now " dust among the dust that once obeyed them."

At Grevenmacher, a little town of three thousand five hundred inhabitants, half hidden in a hollow, the traveller reaches the " bon pays " of the Mosel wine-land, the region producing the rarest wine of this fruitful region. It is a regularly built town, with a spacious " place " in the centre of which is a dis-appointingly insignificant church. Opposite is what was once the castle, now a set of dwelling-houses and once a hospital. In their time the lords of Machern were powerful nobles. Their castle, ruined, is still to be seen a kilometre up-stream opposite Wellen. In the sixteenth and seventeenth centuries, in the wars of the Empire, many were the hosts that assailed the place ; but, as at Remich, peace has driven forth the signs of stormy ages of war. And now the road gets still more interesting and enjoy-able. There are more people about ; life has more in it ; and people must always be the most attractive feature of a country to the stranger. " Verily," as Kipling has said, " there is no life like life on the road—when the skies are cool and all men are kind."

At Mertert the Syre meets the Mosel, and the real wanderer will certainly turn aside to explore that stream. We have already, from the height of Dalheim, looked upon the country in which it has its rise, and if the traveller is inclined to trace his steps back to within sight of the monument there, he will certainly see some most captivating country. And what a string of pretty little villages lie beside that beautiful river ! There is Betzdorf, with its fine modern château ; Schrassich, guarding the gorgeous wooded valley of Birel, with its picturesque castle and mill, and, high above, the ruins of a castle ; Oetrange, a quaint little village ; and, though the list is by no means exhaustive, Contern, most interesting of all. Contern stands a little way from the river, on an imposing eminence. Here, too, Rome camped. Contern was the Imperial Con-ciniacum,[1] it is believed, though some place it at Conz, which, where Sarre and Mosel join, has the remains of a Roman villa. But in the neighbourhood of Contern, too, Roman pillars and sculptures, coins and vases have been unearthed. There is every reason to believe, therefore, that an Imperial villa existed here, where more than one of the Cæsars found rest and quiet, at a spot dominating a wide extent of landscape in which such legions of restful hues march together and there is a peace that comes near to perfection. Later, upon the site of the Roman villa, a castle was built. Remnants of it there are to-day. From pretty Contern to Syren, where the

[1] There are several variations of the name, such as Conciacum, Contionatum and Concionacum.

source of the river is to be found, is a most delightful walk.

Wasserbillig, the next place of importance, has a history which carries it back to the times when Trier was almost another Rome. Constantine's mother made it part of the monastery of St. Maximin, and, well within the city's sphere of influence, it was a centre of religious life. To-day it is a place of another kind. The railway has come and the vineyards are fruitful. Wasserbillig is commercial and prosperous. A railway bridge runs across the river, and a second has taken the place of a fine old structure dating from the fifteenth century. Thus does the need of to-day banish the interesting vestiges of the past. It was a charming old bridge, little more than nine feet wide, and having five curiously unequal arches. At Wasserbillig the wanderer in the Grand Duchy must bid farewell to the Mosel, receiver of all the rivers of Luxembourg save one, and ascend the Sure, along the bank of which a delightful walk of fourteen miles brings him to lovely Echternach.

Time has dealt hardly with relics of the past in that section of the Mosel Valley which forms part of Luxembourg. You leave the past at Sierk, and you live mostly in the present, until, if you follow the Mosel, you reach Igel and Trier. But these are away from our little Grand Duchy. Yet Trier and Mosel were long Rome and Tiber to a great realm, and Echternach and Sure, catching the radiance early, helped in the great work of spreading it abroad. So mounting the Sure, past Born and Wintersdorf and

Rosport, the town which was for centuries a lamp to Luxembourg is reached, and one steps back for a little into " the Past, its ripe plaisance." A little masterpiece of making is Echternach. Protecting heights throw themselves round north and north-east and ward off the coldest winds. Woods are scattered all around, sheltering strange domains which founders of Fairyland might not have made better. A " Little Switzerland " lies round about it ; a beautiful river flows by it. Excepting Luxembourg, no town of the Grand Duchy has such a story to tell ; few places, indeed, have such beauty to show—beauty of vineyard and forest, of orchard and pastures, of mount and vale.

The Escht Hernach of the Celt and the Epterna-cum (doubtless only a villa regia) of the Roman, Echternach really owes its place and fame to neither of these. It comes out of the darkness of Time, a hundred years before the coming of greatness to Charlemagne, two long centuries before the fortress of Luxembourg really began to prepare itself for the battles of long ages. It was an Englishman who lit the lamp of faith in Echternach, one, born by the shores of the Humber, who was of that great band of Englishmen who planted the beacons of faith far and wide upon the Continent. England has all but forgotten her Willibrord ; Rome and Luxembourg count him among the saints. Echter-nach is St. Willibrord's town ; the candle he lighted burned, radiating light and learning, for eleven cen-turies, until the sacrilegious Sansculottes snuffed it out. Just as the seventh century was dying, this

ECHTERNACH, FROM TROOSKNEPCHEN.

Bonaparte of the Bible came to Trier, and from the Princess Irmine, daughter of King Dagobert II, received the little monastery of Echternach, to be a home for the missionaries of the Cross and a refuge for the poor. And just as the baron's castle drew around it the homes of retainers, so the monastery of Echternach, upon which Pope and King showered gifts, attracted many people to the lands it protected, taught them the craft of the soil and in them instilled the faith. But crosier as well as sword may have power in too great a degree. At times the wealth of the monastery bred inside it an undesirable wish for more ; it made the holder of many a sceptre outside envious of such power and riches. So at times crosier and cross were ranged against sword and sceptre—and all suffered. Abbot succeeded abbot from 698 to 1795, till a roll of seventy-one of them was told, and the remains of the first, of the saint, were scattered. And now, for more than a century, the town of St. Willibrord has had no national or spiritual rôle to play. Its glory is no more, but there remains more than a " flickering snatch of memory that floats " in and about it.

The years have not altered Echternach to any very great extent. Still its streets are narrow and rough ; still its houses are quaint and small ; here and there a tradesman's curious sign arrests the eye. Save for a new hotel or two, and modern villas dotted among the clusters of surrounding green, the town has little that is new about it. It is a square town, and the gently flowing Sure flanks it on two sides. Fitting closely into the angle between river and railway is the park, or, as the people call it, " le jardin du casino." And a pleasant little jardin de plaisance it is, too. At the entrance a fountain makes music, throwing sunbeams and spray up almost to the tops of the encircling beeches. What long-past ages seem to find an echo in its song ! In pretty parterres flowers bloom in a bewildering variety of hues ; everywhere trees cast a pleasant, sequin-embroidered shadow on the delightful turf. At the point overlooking the river stands the Louis XV pavilion. From it one can look over the buildings which formed the monastery of old and over the town lying beyond, and up and down the river. The pavilion is, so it is said, the work of the last of the seventy-one abbots. The noise of the first rumblings of the French Revolution had penetrated into the quiet of his domain. He feared the coming of the wreckers ; he wished for a place of repose and contemplation. So he built the picturesque pavilion of prayer, from which he could survey the realm so soon to be wrested from him. The building has, happily, been carefully preserved. That is something to be thankful for, for Echternach has been anything but careful of its rich historical heritage.

From the park the view is charming—the Basilica with its two fine towers, the extensive abbey build-ings, and the parish church of St. Peter and St. Paul standing behind on an eminence. Of this mass of buildings the chief and most interesting is the Basilica of St. Willibrord, in common speech the " Kluster-

kirch " or " église abbatiale." The present building
dates from the eleventh century, the original having
been destroyed half a century before the Norman
Conquest. It was in Roman Gothic style, but the
extensive alterations of 1250 and 1861 have
obliterated many of its characteristics. In the
former year the present roof was added, and the large
windows seen to-day were substituted for the previous
small ones. The French, in 1794, pillaged it and
did great damage, using it as barracks, hospital
and stables. As though that were not vengeance
enough, some of the abbey buildings and the church
were sold—to an earthenware manufacturer ! In
the Basilica this individual erected his furnaces, and
the complete ruin of the building was threatened.
With curious indifference the people of Echternach
stood by and did nothing, till the usual " ligue "
was formed. The "Société pour la Restauration
de la Basilique " did manage to rouse people
to indignation regarding the desecration of the
church, and generous gifts and a Government
grant brought in sufficient funds to enable the
church to be restored to that condition in which we
see it to-day.

The building is very handsome, though the treatment it has received has robbed it of much of its
distinctive style. In spite of that, however, there
is nothing very ugly or unpleasing about it, though
colour has been somewhat lavishly used. High,
narrow and oblong, it has a beautiful interior. There
are two chapels on the south side and one on the
north, and down each side square and round pillars

alternate, the latter with Corinthian capitals. A note-worthy feature is that the choir is lighted by three high windows, of the same description as those to be found in English churches of like age, and occasionally in France. The high altar is particularly beautiful, and the mural decorations tasteful and harmonious. At the entrance to the choir stands the magnificent shrine of St. Willibrord. His ashes, as I have said, were scattered by the French revolutionaries, but, it appears, some of the dust was recovered and found a resting-place below the high altar of the church of St. Peter and St. Paul. In 1906, with the greatest solemnity and pomp, the remains were transferred to the Basilica. The tomb is of Carrara marble, exquisitely carved—a pleasant resting-place for the eyes, which, it must be admitted, at times grow tired of the almost constant red of the interior.

Below the choir is a crypt where can be seen some of the remains of the original eighth-century church. It was there that St. Willibrord was first laid to rest. There are several memorial plaques on the church walls—one concerning the famous Abbot Bertels who wrote the first History of Luxembourg.

The abbey domains, as they can be seen to-day, thrown round the Basilica, buildings and gardens, were the creation, early in the eighteenth century, of the Benedictine abbot Grégoire Schouppe, but they were not destined to remain intact for long. The year 1794 brought desolation here too, and the abbey buildings were subsequently put to various secular uses. The abbey accounts for no less than a quarter of the entire extent of Echternach, and imagination can easily picture the superb place it must have been when the monks were there—the fine buildings, the pavilion, the park, statues, fountains playing among the beeches and the orange-trees. Surely these must have made the place more like a Mansfeld palace than a domain of prayer and service. The splendour has gone. Soldiers of the Revolution drove the monks forth and made barracks of the buildings. To-day, in one part is a girls' school ; in another the gendarmerie are housed. A gymnasium, a dairy, electricity works and some public offices monopolize the rest. There is little to detain one now. Not far away, a minute or two from the entrance to the park, rises the beautiful old church of St. Peter and St. Paul—the parish church. Before climbing the famous staircase the visitor should see St. Willibrord's Hospice. It is opposite the church, this second oldest hospice in all Europe. Here, at least, is something with which Time has been gentle. Before this humble little place even the ruthless Sansculotte put up his sword and bowed his head. Here Time has been guardian angel. And just fancy this : Twelve hundred years ago and more the Abbess Irmine gave this hospice to St. Willibrord, and the saint decided that it would be a home for poor and infirm old men. Such it has been for twelve long centuries, and even to-day the Mother Superior of the quaint old place ministers to the wants of a dozen vieillards, housed in curious, old, small buildings, but happy in the quiet evening

of their lives. And there, too, is a tiny chapel
which must have heard the prayers of the saint.
A soothing place to linger in is this hospice. All
the contemporaries of its earliest years have fallen
before the onslaught of the years save one—the old
Hôtel Dieu in Paris. May that serene haven of
rest ever be there to welcome worn wayfarers ! Near
by, beside the building in which the gendarmerie are
housed, and opposite the hospice, in a grilled grotto
in the rock upon which the church stands, streams
a fountain of water. This is St. Willibrord's Well.
At one time, so it is said, it bubbled up out of the
rock beside the altar in the crypt of the church
above. For a long time the quality of the water
was greatly praised, but a municipality is a coldly
reasoning body, uninfluenced by tradition as a rule.
Above the grotto the City Fathers of Echternach
have placed a notice warning people not to drink
the water.

I like the old parish church of St. Peter
and St. Paul—commonly l'Eglise de Saint-
Pierre—better than the Basilica. It stands on a
" butte " of rock, and doubtless its foundations are
upon a spot where stood a church built in the
very early centuries of the Christian era. In the
Abbess Irmine's time a sacred Christian edifice stood
there. The plateau is shaded by trees, surrounded
by old walls, and reached by stairs from north and
south. The principal approach is the former, a flight
of sixty steps worn by the patient feet of pilgrims,
though now, as I shall presently relate, they come no
longer. The church does not present anything that

is modern to the eye. Viewed from the exterior, though it looks old and somewhat decrepit, the purity of the Roman style in which it is built and its simplicity are at once striking and pleasing. How admirable is its position ! Echternach, the quaint and olden, lies huddled around ; beyond lies a wide extent of wood, pasture, vine and corn lands. Its dark, hoary walls are wrinkled and seared with age, while round it the trees' branches gently wave like the banners in a cathedral. Nor has any one been concerned to give the interior that pomp of colour which has been bestowed upon the Basilica. It remains simple out of the ages, quiet as befits age ; it is whitewashed roughly and almost barn-like in appearance. Echternach and the Church have been niggardly to this holy building, or why that poor wooden altar in shabby Louis XV style? The pulpit and the holy table are also of wood and in the same style, and one turns from them to look at the curious picture on the right of the choir. It dates from 1554, and shows the saint blessing the dancers as they leave the Basilica. Beneath the picture is a sort of cupboard which contains one of the vestments of the saint, his hair shirt and one of the arrows which, it is said, killed St. Sebastian, and which St. Willibrord obtained in Rome. However one may doubt the authenticity of the third relic, there is no reason for being sceptical about the others. Below the high altar is the Roman sarcophagus in which the remains of St. Willibrord rested until 1906. Truly there are not many churches which have preserved, as has done that of St. Peter and St. Paul, their simplicity and venerableness. So it wins a regard, in those who know it, never attained by proudest art and most pompous ritual.

Echternach is widely famous for the great dancing procession which takes place in the town every Whitsun Tuesday. Annually this curious rite draws to the town about twenty thousand " pilgrims " and probably as many more spectators. These come from far and near. The origin of this dance is lost in the mists of the ages, and though it is mentioned for the first time in records bearing a date as late as the end of the sixteenth century, there is little reason to believe that this singular ceremony was not held for a considerable period prior to that. Pilgrimages to the tomb of Saint Willibrord began early in the eighth century, very soon after the demise of the saint. From those pilgrimages doubtless the dancing procession was evolved. Tradition has it that the evolution was fairly rapid, and that before the eighth century had waned it was already the great religious ceremony of Echternach. An epizootic distemper, it is said, seized the cattle in the neighbourhood, and the people, distressed at seeing the animals frantic and in convulsions, turned to the shrine of the saint with their prayers and offerings. A homœopathy of faith made them proceed dancing to the tomb. Their faith had its reward ; the animals all got well. Authorities civil and religious have often endeavoured to put a stop to the ceremony, which lent itself to abuses, but only on one occasion did they succeed. And then the disease reappeared amongst the cattle.

So it has been held ever since. Now, however, though the form of old is preserved, it is not so much the welfare of the animals that the dancers are concerned about. They hope to propitiate the spirit which sends convulsive ailments to mankind. They dance for personal reasons, and they can dance by deputy. One member of a family may represent all the others ; a boy may dance for his bedridden grandmother.

Religious dancing is very old, but now it only exists in odd corners of Europe. It is likely to live for a long time yet in Echternach, for the people do not give the slightest sign of becoming " modern " enough to disbelieve in this ancient rite. On the Prussian side of the river, beyond the bridge, at the old cross where the four roads meet, the thousands of dancers, old, middle-aged and young, male and female, assemble early in the morning. At eight o'clock, after a sermon in the open air, the great Maximilian bell in the parish church steeple tolls— that is the signal for the procession to start. (The bell, by the way, was presented to Echternach by the Emperor Maximilian in 1512 in remembrance of his pilgrimage to St. Willibrord's tomb in that year. It weighs about three and a half tons.) The dancers begin to fall into line. At the head are the clergy, chanting, and following them comes the long file of dancers, singers, praying pilgrims and musicians in no settled order, the musicians being scattered along the whole length of the procession. On the bridge the dance begins, opened by a number of boys. It is a curious movement to the accompani-

ment of this age-old, polka-like tune, played on a
great variety of instruments :—

The movement consists of taking five steps forwards and then three backwards ; the motion is
slow and sedate, and it is a most curious sight to
see the swaying procession wending its way slowly

through the streets. The distance to be covered, from the bridge to the Basilica, is scarcely three-quarters of a mile, yet it takes five or six hours for the entire procession to pass over the route. Until a few years ago—up to the time of the removal of St. Willibrord's tomb to the Basilica—the dancers proceeded to the church of St. Peter and St. Paul where the remains of the saint lay. To reach that church a flight of sixty steps must be climbed, and to climb it in the way mentioned was certainly a test of physical endurance after five or six hours of " dancing." In 1906, however, the tomb of the saint was removed to the Basilica, and there the procession now comes to its end, without any such final feat of strength. The dancers pass before the tomb, place their offerings before it, and then leave the church. In 1912 it is said that 22 banner-carriers, 119 priests, 357 musicians, 3,913 singers, 3,402 praying pilgrims and 12,163 dancers took part in the procession, a total of 19,976.

Though certainly picturesque, the procession un-doubtedly has its painful and objectionable features. It is pitiful to see a lot of old and infirm people, who should be at home, struggling along in this painful manner. Most of them, indeed, fall out long before the end. The ceremony, however, is one which will die hard ; every year it appears to grow more popular, though, of course, it can scarcely be denied that religion becomes ever a lesser factor in making people join in it. For the occasion Echternach is always gaily decorated. The windows of all the houses are brightened with flowers ; flags

and streamers float in the air. As for the crowds
of spectators, it is a marvel where they all come
from. People line the streets thickly on both sides,
and those who do not take part in the procession
or fill the passive rôle of spectators crowd the
churches of the town from as early an hour as
five o'clock. Early in the afternoon, when the
ceremony has concluded, a fair begins, and merriment is the order for the rest of the day among the
crowds in the streets, while stall and sideshow and
roundabout provide amusements until late at night,
with a fainter echo on the following day.

Echternach's quiet, narrow old streets radiate from
a spacious market-place, and there is to be seen one
of the most curious buildings in the Duchy. It is
the Dingstuhl, perhaps the most interesting and distinctive relic of the Middle Ages that exists. The
style is Gothic, and the date of construction must be
placed somewhere about the middle of the fifteenth
century. It has recently been very admirably
restored. The ground floor consists of an open hall
or arcade, above which are two stories, the roof
having two large and half a dozen small turrets.
The face of the building, which protrudes considerably in front of those beside it, is decked with six
statues, of nobody in particular, I believe, and the
delightfully fine sculpture at the tops of the windows
must attract attention. In common speech, the
Dingstuhl is the "Denzelt." The name Dingstuhl,
of course, is derived from "dingen," to deliberate,
and "Stuhl," seat. It was, therefore, the place for
the meeting of the local council, where justice was

THE DINGSTUHL, ECHTERNACH.

To face p. 156.

administered by the City Fathers, over whom presided the mayor, or Schultheiss. Yearly a curious gathering took place in the hall. It was the Jahrgeding. All the freemen of the city were bound to attend, and the local by-laws were read over to them. These fixed the rights of the burghers and the various punishments to be inflicted for wrongdoing. The city magistrates in olden days were the servants of the Abbey. In the Basilica they were required to take solemn oath of allegiance to the Abbot. At that time the Dingstuhl contained the prison and, for a long period, the chamber of torture. The local council still holds its meetings in the building.

Opposite the Dingstuhl is the old Hôtel de Ville, which in Echternach, and in Trier as well, has the popular description of " Unter den Steilen " —" Under the Pillars "—on account of the fact that its ground floor is in the form of an arcade or open hall, very similar to that of the Dingstuhl. But it has not been so well preserved. Private persons have come into possession and have carried out building alterations which have nearly swept away the original character of the building. Here, in days of old, the representatives of the trade guilds, with the Stadtbaumeister at their head, met and deliberated, and in the arcade were the shops and stalls of traders. It will be noticed that the style of each of the five remaining pillars differs. The reason is that each was designed by a different trade guild, and those standing to-day are said to have been put up by the butchers, bakers, fishers, merchants and smiths.

Early one morning, just when the softness of the first sunshine was being thrown over all, I left Echternach and climbed up Troosknepchen to the well-worn pavilion there. It is a most beautiful spot, glorious with blossom and blade, around which the floating hair of trees is blown about the skies and the halcyon breath of morning is good as new wine. There one sees best of all the immortal loveliness of Echternach, lying well protected in a widened valley of deepest translucent green. Its pristine glory is departed ; its warfare is accomplished. But still there is something strangely alluring in the place ; it is curiously fascinating to look down upon the little town which for long centuries was a lamp to the feet of so many, where an English saint fought his fights for the Cross, where a glorious abbey sprang up rich and powerful beyond the dreams of avarice, its glory and the even tenor of its way often disturbed and finally swept away by the sword. Still there is much to recall the days of old ; there is a remnant of greatness ; there is the full meed of peace. Out of this subdued little city of memories, many things that were precious mingle " with the dust of alien things " ; but memories are, after all, possessions beyond price —they are the spirit of a place. Echternach has them in fullest measure, and she will

Hold for ever sacro-sanct
Such dewy memories as these.

LITTLE SWITZERLAND

In woods men feel: in towns they think.

ALFRED AUSTIN.

At a leap
Thou shalt strike a woodland path,
Enter silence, not of sleep,
Under shadows, not of wrath.

GEORGE MEREDITH.

CHAPTER V

LITTLE SWITZERLAND

ECHTERNACH seems to attract the modern tourist to a degree which is not excelled by any other part of the Grand Duchy of Luxembourg. Yet, I think, there is no part of our little Ruritania which is so slightly known as that curious and beautiful region which lies between Echternach and the Erenz Noire —the " little Switzerland " of the country, as it has most appropriately and justly been called. And the reason, I am sure, is this. The district cannot be properly explored save afoot, and that by rough tracks and forest paths. Motor-car and bicycle must remain on the outskirts of this most entrancing piece of country, and they and the railway will not help visitors for more than a mile or two here and there. Unless they travel light, the " little Switzerland " must remain terra incognita to the wanderers. Go afoot, and if kilometres in goodly number do not frighten you, then in " Nature's infinite book of secrecy " you will read a little more.

One beautiful summer day I was fortunate enough to be asked to join a motor-car party travelling from Remich to Echternach. I say fortunate enough, because, knowing the intervening country, I was in a hurry to reach Echternach, where there was still a good deal for me to explore. In a few hours we were carried from one town to the other. That was bad enough for the others, who were visiting the country for the first time, and it appeared to me to be something akin to sacrilege to rush in a cloud of dust at many miles an hour along that most glorious of rivers, Schiller's "Virgin of Lorraine." But worse than that was still to come. We arrived at Echternach late in the afternoon, and in the morning I asked my friends what their plans were. Oh, they were going on to Vianden ; there was only one road fit for the car, so that it was all that was to be done. They wanted me to come farther with them, but my excuse was that there were roads round about Echternach to keep me busy and happy for weeks.

Probably the remaining part of this book would be insufficient to do the full justice they deserve to the beauties and curiosities of the Echternach region. I shall, therefore, have to pick and choose in my wanderings, and leave to any one who may be following where I went something to discover for himself. There is certainly not in Europe a more extraordinary rock region than that at the gates of which we now stand. It is as though some vast pagan frieze had been scattered over it in disarray, the gauds of some long-vanished might of art or religion, the mighty cenotaphs of a faith whose light has long been spent, the victims of a devastating shock which the kindly Mother Earth has not yet had time to cover with her mantle.

It is, of course, the sea which has given us this majestic region of mass and music—river and wind music—this rock symphony, Strauss in stone. Above it the ocean waves once rolled to beat on the shore near Brandenbourg and Vianden. Cleft and cavern once made the " dark, unfathomed caves of ocean." Now they are high and dry, great and narrow pathways through rock-heart, where sometimes there is not room for two persons to pass, deep, dark caverns into the earth, winding stairs through labyrinths, where even on the hottest summer day the air is icy cold. The gigantic maze would please Reinhardt, and in it the imagination of Conan Doyle or H. G. Wells might find places which would serve as the scenes for works of weird imagination. Sometimes a narrow way through the rock will carry the wanderer up to a high rock's top, offer him a gorgeous view, and then quickly carry him down again into an abyss strange with the awesomeness of another world.

The greatest glory of the region is the Müllerthal, which is the valley of the Erenz Noire, the charming river of which we shall see something in our wander across country to Mersch, as its waters ripple and sing through the Blumenthal. The quick and easy way to reach the valley from Echternach is, of course, to go by train to Grundhof, where the Erenz Noire pours its waters into the Sure, and then ascend the valley by the excellent main road. Those who take that route are beyond advice.

It was a German student—" sechs Schmisse zierten seine Wang' "—who enticed me up to the pavilion.

I presumed he wished me to come there because he had the general German weakness for such erections on points of vantage, but the spirit of "Die alte Burschenherrlichkeit" led us on in company from point to point, until ten hours later we found ourselves engaging a room together at Grundhof. A German is a good wanderer in other countries. As an emigrant he drops his nationality with a rapidity which has always been remarkable. Probably the reason is that he is more sensitive than are others to the patriotism of the place in which he finds himself. And here was the student already not far removed from being a patriotic Luxembourger. He had fished down Alzette and up Our ; he knew the history of the country from its stormy youth, and no one Duchy-born could have been more enthusiastic about the little country's glories. And discussing them we reached the pavilion from which we had what we thought would be our last view— and a delightful one it was—of Luxembourg's little Rome.

Then you plunge into the forest, and soon the first scouts of Rockland are encountered, massive boulders scattered on either side of the path. A few minutes later you stand at the entrance to the Wolfsschlucht, one of the hugest and most curious of the gorges of this region. The cleft in the great rock is, roundly, a score of feet wide, and down into it a rough stairway leads ; 150 feet high, the rock faces tower on either side, and, scattered here and there, flowers and bushes find a foothold. Guarding this gorge stands a most extraordinary obelisk, reminding one

THE WOLFSSCHLUCHT.

(Echternach and the Sure in the background)

To face p. 138.

of Cleopatra's Needle. This " flèche " and the faces of the rocks have been cunningly carved by the elements, but they look as though Ung of old here, too, had been busy with his rough chisel and his hammer. Push on—it's rough going !—through the gorge, which is over 150 yards long, and the deeper the visitor penetrates into it the more like a feudal castle in ruins does the appalling confusion of rock become. Then on the left another minor gorge will be seen. It is the Teufelsschart, or Devil's Cleft. By going through it and scrambling upwards the top of the greatest of the rocks is reached, and a little rough manœuvring will bring you to a spot from which you see distant Echternach in the frame of the Wolfsschlucht. The river leads the eye away to Prussian Weilerbach, with its factories, and to still more distant wooded Bollendorf.

The woodland path descends ; it crosses the Hegelbach, and quickly comes within earshot of the faint music of the Aesbach, a little stream which, for some kilometres, entangles itself with the roadway and in the deep, silent little pools of which trout wax fat. Soon comes another giant's handful of rocks, a massive maze called " the Labyrinth." It looks like a pigmies' town turned, for some stupendous sin of the little people, into imprisoning boulders. Still streets and ruelles are there in bewildering number, and in this rock-town it is easy to lose oneself.

Just as we had left the dwarfs' town another German, facially " adorned " in the same manner as my companion, with Rücksack, a knickerbocker suit of tweeds, the pattern for which must have been a

caricature of John Bull in *Ulk* or *Simplicis-
simus*, with a huge pipe and a thick stick, met us,
coming from the right. We saluted him with
" Guten Tag ! " and passed on, going straight ahead.
Half a minute later a loud voice came from behind
us : " Rechts gehen ! Rechts gehen ! " We turned
and saw the huge pipe and the thick stick being
flourished in front of the check suit. " Sie müssen
rechts gehen ! Rechts gehen ! " There was evidently something the matter, so when pipe and stick
no longer gyrated in a manner to make approach
a matter of danger we spread out a huge map and
consulted our stentorian adviser, who would certainly
have made a champion club-swinger.

On the map he traced a new path for us, first
along the Halsbach, which, near where we were
standing, came to join the Aesbach, and then towards
the Sure, parallel to the way by which we had
come, finally reaching our path about half a mile
to the rear. The German could flourish long descriptive adjectives with the same facility as that
with which he swung his pipe and stick. The idea
that we should miss the Welkeschkammer and
Geierslay, to say nothing of Zigeunerlay, was " über-
haupt dumm." They were " grossartig," " kolossal,"
" reizend," " herrlich," " fabelhaft," and worthy at
least of twenty other adjectives. He was going
to the Labyrinth, would wait there till we came
round, and accompany us to Berdorf, where he had
found an inn to his liking.

Near where Aesbach and Halsbach join stands
Le Pérékop, one of the mightiest rocks of this region,

a rough mass parted in the middle, so that there is
a " couloir " up which it is possible to struggle to
the top, an admirable view-point. German Student
Number Two had just come down when we encountered him, and Number One and I both knew it
of old. So we passed it by this time, noting no
difference on its weather-worn face. We turned to
the right and plunged into the narrow glade through
which Halsbach sings to join the almost silent
Aesbach in order, it would seem, to teach it how
to sing. Trees huddle closely together about the
path ; mosses, grasses and flowers nearly succeed
in obscuring the way ; an almost excluded sun lets
twilight reign ; no human hand has sought to introduce order in this " bee-loud glade." An obligingly
placed sign-post, however, soon tells you that it is
no virgin forest you are exploring. An arrow points
the way to the Welkeschkammer—that is, the buckwheat depot. The way is an extremely stiff one,
and it leads to the depot, which is in the form of
a sort of dungeon in the rock, 4 or 5 feet from
floor to ceiling, and in size about 12 by 16 feet.
Who kept buckwheat here I confess I don't know,
but after the long sojourn in the shade it is pleasant
to see once more a sunny landscape, which you can
through openings in the rock ; a delightful landscape it is, covered with " a veil of versicoloured
light." Here we were high above the topmost
branches of the trees, in a curious, cool retreat from
which only the arrangement to meet the other German
drove us all too soon.

Quite close by is another curious rock formation

called the Zigeunerlay, or the Rock of the Bohemian. There is a huge grotto, the overhanging stone being of the most bizarre shape, and in it stand table and chairs of stone. It is said, though I am not sure with complete truth, that it got its name from a Prussian who exiled himself here in order to escape from military service during the Franco-Prussian War.

On through the forest we went, after some care,-less wandering, by a path leading eastwards again, a way which we had some difficulty in finding. Two woodland ways, it appears, run up the Halsbach valley, and the path we searched for cuts off from that on the left bank. It leads along the top of the wooded embankment on the left side of the Aesbach, twists and turns, until, within but a short distance of the Sure, the Geierslay is reached.

The name means " Rock of Vultures," and the " massif," with the usual pavilion on the top, stands prominently alone, the highest point on the plateau, wedged in between Sure and Aesbach. There is no finer view-point anywhere in this region, and we felt very friendly towards Student Number Two who had set us on the way to find it. It is easily reached from Echternach—the town makes a charming picture seen from the top of the rock—by taking the main road along the Sure's right bank and then that which branches off where the Aesbach goes under road and rail to join the larger river. From the rock we descended quickly to the Aesbach path, and were soon at the Labyrinth, where we found Student Number Two contentedly swinging his stick as he sat upon one of the rocks upon which he had carved his initials.

Off we went in single file along the narrow path by the Aesbach. Sometimes the tiny brook hummed gently through grassy and mossy surroundings ; at others it was merely a string of crystal-clear pools scattered twistingly among the rocks. Soon we came across a gigantic triple grotto, one huge open chamber and two smaller and dark ones. This is La Hollay, the Hollow Rock, which a few years ago was difficult of access, but now the path makes it quite easy to reach. Tradition has it that the Romans ground their corn here, and it is said that the circular cuttings on walls and roof are caused by their chiselling grind-stones from the rock. But why, in this rock-rich region, the Roman, who was a practical person, should put up a scaffold and carve a piece out of the ceiling for the purpose is somewhat obscure. It seems going so far out of the way to find hard and unnecessary work. Neither can I believe that the Romans carried their corn to this outlandish forest hermitage to grind it. No ; some other people, I am sure, hollowed this rock, or increased the size of the natural grotto they found, for the cavern has clearly been cut by some one and is not natural as seen to-day.

The vast rock is moss-covered. From the largest entrance to the farthest inner point is between 70 and 80 feet, and the broadest part of the interior about 40. Pillars, hanging between roof and floor as waterspouts between cloud and sea, have been left as supports. The walls and parts of the roof are covered with carved and painted initials, while numerous bold inscriptions tell of the visits of various associations—choirs, tourist societies, this, that and the other association have placed there the fairly durable record of their sojourn in this cool cave. Some ought really to have been charged a feu-duty, so great is the area they have monopolized, and all should have been prevented from doing it.

"But at any rate," declared Student Number Two, "here is an interesting inscription." And he pointed to one high up on the rock outside the cavern. It is one of those puzzle inscriptions of which the Luxembourger is so fond, and it is in German as follows :—

> Herzliches Vivat !
> Einer hohen Regierung
> welche diese sehenswerthen Sch
> luchten & Hohlwege
> dem Publicum zugaenglich
> gemacht hat
> Die Jugend von Berdorf.
> MDCCCLXXX

Die Jugend von Berdorf delivers its praise in a puzzle ; it puts the laurel crown it awards in a maze. If you read the letters which are underlined, you find the name Eischen (which, by the way, should really be Eyschen), Paul, otherwise his Excellency Monsieur Paul Eyschen, Minister of State, who during his tenure of office has done much to open up the wonders and curiosities of this region to those who wander in it.

A few minutes after leaving the Hollow Rock

the path conducts the wanderer from the forest's shades and leads him across fields to Berdorf, a village straggling for about half a mile along a road at right angles to our path. It has about seven or eight hundred inhabitants, a long row of houses, broken only by its church, a building roofed with slates and whitewashed, an ordinary enough village were it not for two things. In the first place it stands high in Sonne und Luft, 1,000 feet up on a plateau ringed round by the green of woods, breathing an air which is ether. I fancy that when the sea swept over this region Berdorf was an islet looking over the waves to its neighbour Beaufort.

German Student Number Two led us to a little hotel near the church and invited us to lunch. Then we discovered that he had been en villégiature here for three weeks, leisurely appreciating the charms of the neighbourhood, but never straying far from the good air of Berdorf. Here we enjoyed the Simple Life with good cookery, which is the Simple Life as it should be. And we certainly found this high-placed little village a most restful and quiet little spot. Out in the fields—oh, but they were like those in " Sussex by the sea " !—the men and women of Berdorf find their work, and during most of the day the little place is deserted save for the children looking after children not much smaller.

The second thing of interest in Berdorf is the parish church. Not that it is old or that in itself it is interesting, for not only is it plain but it is comparatively new and almost wholly unadorned.

But it has one treasure. It is the altar of the four deities, a splendidly preserved piece of Roman work, the stone for which an old village worthy, who showed us the altar enclosed in a wooden covering, told us was taken from the Hollow Rock. The four deities are Hercules, Apollo, Juno and Minerva. Each has one side of the altar. Hercules is in front, with club and lion-skin ; at the rear is Juno, holding shell and sceptre. Apollo, with lyre, bow and quiver, is on the left, and on the opposite side is armed Minerva. The altar is about 4 feet high and each relief about 3 feet square. It is one of the finest Roman relics I saw in Luxembourg.

Where the altar of the four deities was found I was unable to discover. But within comparatively recent years it seems to have changed its abode several times. I could trace its wanderings no farther back than to a little church, now gone, near Müllerthal village, an edifice said to have been one of St. Willibrord's numerous churches. It came to Berdorf before the parish church was built, and served as altar in the old building in which the people worshipped. The parish church was erected about eighty-five years ago, and in it the altar was placed. In the old church, so our worthy told us, there were many very ancient relics, but he had no idea where they were now. Probably they are classified, catalogued and numbered in more than one museum, and it is satisfactory that at least one has not had to submit to that fate. The altar of the four deities is regarded by the Berdorf people with something akin to awe ; they hold it in great reverence, and that is probably what has saved it for them and their little church.

It was hard to leave quiet little Berdorf, and indeed the sun was well on its afternoon journey before we parted from Student Number Two, went across the fields beyond Berdorf, and took a twisting way through the woods and towards the Sure. We reached the little narrow and quiet valley where the Roitzbach has its rise and into which a shower of stupendous rocks has been thrown. Then, disregarding the sign-post which tells us that Höhl, or Hell, is reached by the path to the left—I reserved that path for to-morrow—we went to the right into a little region of delightful beauty. On one side rise stern-faced and pointed rocks, which sea-waves only could have carved ; on the left the land, beautifully wooded, slopes away gently to the last miles of the Erenz Noire. The Berdorf-Grundhof main road cuts across our path, having forced a way through the rocky barrier along which is our track. Crossing it we soon reach the ravine which the Wanterbach has cut to find the Erenz Noire.

This is a wild little corner, and for more than an hour we stayed marvelling at the extraordinary variety of shape which the huge rocks display, and wandered about till we found a resting-place for another hour, at the spot where the Wanterbach throws itself over a rocky precipice and forms one of the most remarkable cascades I have ever seen. Its white spray was exquisitely embroidered with rainbow-ribbons and sun sequins, while light and shade wove lovely lace upon its disarray.

And another marvel is not far away. It is the Sept Gorges, variously described locally as Sieben-schlüff, Sievenschlüff or Sieweschlüff. Imagine a huge rock, say like that upon which Stirling Castle stands, thrown high in the air and then scattering in great fragments on falling earth again. Only in that way, one thinks, could the Sept Georges have come into existence. Seven of the separating gorges are large enough to permit people to walk through them—narrow " couloirs " communicating with one another, walled high on either side. Then there comes a stairway, cut roughly out of the rock, by which the top is reached, to show the climber the valleys of Erenz Noire and Sure at his feet.

Leaving Sept Gorges, the path picks its way among giant rocks along the edge of the Berdorf plateau, which at this point pushes itself out into the angle formed by the junction of Erenz Noire and Sure. The track gradually rises until the imposing group of rocks called Kasselt is reached. On its high summit the red, white and blue of Luxembourg floated lazily in the evening breeze, and we climbed to the platform on which the flagstaff has been erected. No words can adequately describe the delightful view to be seen from here—a " memory of show and scent." Silvery Sure advances twist-ing in front, turns to gold as it flows past, and then disappears in a proud and gracious sweep away to the right. Beaufort lies in the distance to the left, and far away the Our valley is visible, threaded by its lovely stream ; below lies Grundhof, from which the noise of the whistle and snorting of engines

THE ENTRANCE TO HÖHL.

To face p. 149.

ascends—the only sounds that cleave the summer evening silence. Behind, forests sweep across the plateau to a distant horizon upon which the sunset hangs out its blazing banner. It is a gorgeous evening spectacle.

We descended quickly to Grundhof, and, as we had been ten hours on the way, sought the inn and ordered dinner. Grundhof lies at the end of the valley of the Erenz Noire. Where the engines of this busy little junction steam and smoke the once riotous river slips gently into the Sure. The little village has no history ; road, river and railway come to it in triple file from both sides. Its importance is largely industrial, for it has a railway bringing down to it the produce of the great quarries of Dillingen and Reisdorf ; the wanderer knows it as standing at the entrance to one of the most glorious of Ruritania's valleys—that of the Erenz Noire— which rises in the Grunenwald, that beautiful forest spreading itself on the outskirts of the Duchy's capital.

" There's a fine road up the valley," said Madame of the inn, and we set off, adieux said to three delightful little children, whose grief it was that the automatic machine on the veranda had been emptied by them overnight with our pennies, despite the warning that it was always well to leave something for the morning.

" We'll have to return by this road," remarked the student. " That's a nuisance, isn't it ? " he added, true wanderer that he was.

" Well, then, what about that path we passed

yesterday leading to Höhl? It's almost certain to lead parallel to this."

We spread out our map, which did not show Höhl, but a farmer's boy at a farm near by told us that if we struggled up the tiny river which was rippling into the Erenz Noire not far away we should come to the spot which we desired to reach, and the path would lead us to Müllerthal village. So we crossed the river by the bridge at the farm and followed the path until we came upon the tributary, the Roitzbach, along whose scanty and placid waters we went. It was comparatively easy going, though at times steep, and breath-taking detours were necessary. We were not long, however, in striking the spot where on the previous day we had turned to the right, where Roitzbach cuts a valley into the plateau towards Berdorf.

Here we met two German Pfaffen, who, having come from Höhl, had lost their bearings. We put them on the unorthodox way for their destination— Echternach.

"You are doing this journey in the proper direction," said one. "Höhl, then the Eisgrotte. We did the Eisgrotte first, which is a mistake." We showed correct appreciation of the somewhat heavy Germanic humour.

Höhl was not far away. Rocks and flowers dispute for first place in one's memory along the twisting path, and then suddenly you come across a darksome cavity in the rock. It is Hell. Some one had most obligingly left at the entrance a piece of candle attached to a stick. Lighting it, we descended into the deeps. For nearly two hundred feet the dark passage leads gently downward into the rock's heart. At times one has to stoop to get along ; at others the vault of the roof is many yards above. All the way the passage is narrow ; there is just enough room for two people to pass each other. It is said that this is a natural cavern, that no blasting has been resorted to in order to make or extend it, and I think appearances bear out the statement. It is one of the most eerie spots of this rock-region—one of the most curious of all its wonders. Equally marvellous, though of a different description, is the Schnellert, about half an hour farther on. To reach it the path first ascends by a long stairway and then falls again, leading to a mass of rock similar to the Sept Gorges. The huge rocks are thrown about in the most extraordinary confusion, some of them rising to enormous heights and shutting out the sunlight ; narrow ways run everywhere, in some of which the hand of man is evident in the making. But he has done nothing in vandal style ; all he has done is to make it but a little easier to wander about in this awe-inspiring chaos of cliffs.

Groups of rocks follow one another in quick succession. Next comes the Binzeltschlüff. Here the pathway has been driven by man, but in extremely clever and artistic fashion. Steep, narrow, twilight-shrouded ruelles make one fancy that here is a corner of earth struck with barrenness, so grim are the bare rocks among which the way twists. Then suddenly you come upon a fine piece of road-making. Right through the stupendous cliffs a splendid main road has been cut, leading from Berdorf to the Müllerthal road. Crossing this road one dives again into the dim, hidden, steep pathways and deep gorges. Surely some of the caverns to be seen must have sheltered the ancient Celt. Sometimes, at any rate, there are found here axe and arrow heads such as he used. The Wehrschrumschlüff follows soon, another rock-labyrinth distinguished by a gigantic verdure-covered peak which rises high above the others and the topmost branches of the trees as well. Then for a time the going is more gentle by a charming woodland path, until, about twenty minutes later, a way leads off on the left. It is to the Eisgrotte, the Cavern of Ice. The place well deserves its name ; so deep and narrow are its gorges, overhung with close foliage, that they are cool as deep cellars.

By this time it was approaching midday, and the German was thinking very seriously of lunch.

" We don't want to hurry on to Müllerthal village," he said ; " that should be done leisurely. What about Consdorf? Look "—and he pointed to his well-thumbed map—" there a road loses itself in that farm not far off. Let's try and find it."

We pushed on, then, beyond the Eisgrotte, and soon came out upon a field across which was the farm—called Dostert, by the way. We found the road, the farm people confirming the directions of the map by saying that it led directly to Consdorf. Over the Dosterbach we went, past another farm, and then through a wood from the southern side of which Consdorf was not far distant. At the Hotel Mersch Madame attended to us in true Luxembourg

KOHLSCHEUER, MÜLLERTHAL.

style, and when the heat of the day had passed
we left the village to seek the only two remaining
clusters of rocks which we had left unexplored.

At the southern extremity of the village an obliging
rustic went out of his way to guide us to the proper
path, and in little more than half an hour we reached
the valley of the Hertbour, on the left wall of which
a path leads first to the Kohlscheuer and then, a few
minutes later, to the Déwepetz.

In spite of all that we had seen in Post-Impres-
sionist rock-effects, the Kohlscheuer surprised us.
A winding way and at times a rustic stair lead to it,
an enormous heap of gigantic rocks, regarded by
many as the most extraordinary of the whole region.
It is difficult to leave this curious stony maze, this
remarkable confusion, with its narrow clefts, deep
and highly walled. The visitor will spend at least
an hour here ; he cannot help himself, so curious
is the place.

Little sweeping curves lead to the Déwepetz—the
name means " the deep wells." This curiosity consists of two narrow galleries through a massive rock,
from one of which another " couloir " runs. We
followed our track on leaving it for about half an
hour, turning gradually round towards the Erenz
Noire, the valley of the Hertbour widening considerably as it approached the Müllerthal.

" Can there be," asked my companion, " anything
to equal or excel what we have already seen? " He
was anxious to cut down to the main road—
Echternach-Müllerthal—and to reach the delightful
valley as soon as possible. He allowed himself to

be persuaded, however, that the good wine might possibly be kept to the last, and that it was not wise to skip the final chapter of the book of chaos.

So we reached the Goldfralay, the name akin in meaning to Lorelei—the Rock of the Golden Lady. If it lacks the greatness and grandeur of the Rhine rock, it has an impressiveness of its own. It towers more than a hundred feet high, and passages split it into four. The legend attached to it is similar to that connected with the Lorelei.

You enter by a huge natural portal, and the cleft gradually gets narrower and narrower, until, as one goes along, sleeves rub upon the rock-walls on either side. Up and up the passage goes, at places the way being improved by rough steps, until the top of the giant rock is reached. It is a fairly extensive platform, covered with beautiful mosses and shrubs. Here beautiful purple heather grows and flowers of many kinds, including the blue-bells of—Luxembourg. Squirrels come up by way of the trees and play about in frisky and friendly manner, often coming near to inspect the person who has discovered their high-pitched forest home. And what a glorious view there is from here, lifted high above the topmost leaves of a great forest ! Deep down in the valley the Biresbach lies hidden in its trees ; Consdorf stands high on the opposite plateau. And in autumn that great extent of undulating woodland is beautiful beyond all description ; the first leaves are falling, and the foliage is of every tint from freshest green to gold and from gold to deepest brown—a marvellous mosaic. A mill squatting in the valley, the high church tower at Consdorf, the dim outline of the houses of the village—these alone break but slightly the ocean of trees spreading as far as the eye can reach. And, like a ring of darkened colour on a sunlit sea, you can trace, very faintly, that semicircle of rocks which we have explored, a rampart facing the Sure, but a rampart over which peace has spread its mantle.

Down again reluctantly we went. A few minutes later we passed the Goldkaul, the " trench of gold," so called, I should think, because of the yellowish tint of the rock and because sulphuret of copper used to be extracted here. Then comes the last fort of the rampart wall.

It is the Eulenburg, the Castle of the Owls. And it is appropriately named. The dusk had come down when we reached it, and already the eerie, mournful calls of the shy lords of this castle could be heard. If you would see the landscape bathed in twilight, climb to the top of the largest rock. From it you can look right down the Müllerthal to Grundhof ; on the left Beaufort stands on its eminence, and all around the darkening forest with its glades. Through fissures we scrambled in the gloom till we got clear of the awesome rocks. The extreme narrowness of the passages and their extraordinary length is what makes the Owls' Castle different from all the other forts of the long rampart of rock, the end of which we have now reached.

We went through the woods, a short cut, and saw an hotel sign which marked the end of our long forest ramble.

The Müllerthal — the Millers' Dale ! What
memories of peace, of scenic charm, of joyful riot
of waters, of chaos of rock, of beauty of flower
and tree the name recalls to him who has sought
the Schiessentümpel from placid Grundhof ! Coming
up the fertile and luxuriant valley, the wanderer
passes from Nature's peace to her passion and back
again ; it is as though one came and went from
before the pictures of an East or Waterlow to the
challenging canvases of an Impressionist. And Erenz
Noire ! Fair the river is, and black only when rocks
throw their great gloom upon her clear waters.
But black goes well with some colours. She is a
white danseuse who for some of her fairy frolics
chooses a black background, and will have
Wagnerian, nay, Straussian music to foot it to.
Into parts of the valley the world-maker has thrown
all that there is of the bizarre and the beautiful—
tower and cavern, rampart and pillar ; he exhausts
shape and form and effect ; he touches the utmost
limit of chisel-work and hammer-labour. Since
the beginning water—rain and river—has laboured,
and endlessly it still labours, carving this wondrous
work.

Up, high up, on the valley sides wind and rain
are still the architects of this stupendous art. Little
by little, slowly, they complete little fragments of it
and hurl them downward to the stream for the waters
to play with and to work more harmoniously into the
Dantesque scheme of things. How well the stream
does its work ! It makes stepping-stones, pool-
guards, trout-shelters of them ; it covers them with

THE SCHIESSENTÜMPEL, MÜLLERTHAL.

ever-living moss, a roothold for fern and flower,
throws a cascade of its fair waters over them, or
rings them round with river-plants which have their
root in its bed. And hazel and pine make of its
home an arbour, mint the sunshine for it to spend
in the gloom, and deliver the rain gently to it. Erenz
Noire has made the valley fruitful. Men have built
mills by its side and by that of its dozen tributaries
from ‘Müllerthal village to Grundhof. With strength
of these waters “ Ferme ” and “ Mühle ” have
prospered.

A little above the village is to be seen its masterpiece—the Schiessentümpel, or Schiesztümpel, or a
score of other spellings. Several great rocks have
sought to bar the waters’ way, but the stream has
forced itself between them, and now we see one of
the most charming little cascades one could wish to
behold, several thick threads of white falling into
a silvery pool giving the alert trout a good run before
their jump to that above. The surroundings are
most charming. An old bridge spans the cascade,
its stones artistically carved to look like logs of
wood ; paths lead up and down stream in the
encircling woodland.

Of such is the Millers’ Dale—alternate peace and
war. But it is ever beautiful.

Turn your back on Müllerthal and you are back
in the land of castles and romance. The Kasselbach
runs into the Erenz Noire just at the entrance to
the village as the wanderer comes up the valley.
This is a riotous stream which has cut a picturesque
valley for itself out of the green plateau edged with

the silver of Erenz and Hallerbach. On the hilly spur which drives a wedge into the corner of Erenz Noire and Kasselbach stands, visible from afar, the strange and eerie ruin of Heringerburg. The ruin is almost at its last stage of form, a grim heap of stones which have yielded to what must have been a long assault of Nature's fury upon this verdant height. From the disorder—one wall still stands— you can gather but little to tell you what this stronghold was like in the days of old, but, having powerful neighbours, no doubt here dwelt a seigneur of consequence.

And, I think, it must be the oldest of all castle ruins, for you do not go to the written pages of history to learn Heringerburg. The pages of romance are what you must turn ; you must listen to tradition's tale. Tenth century is the date generally associated with its building, and its builders are said to have been the Heringer, an unruly tribe of Saxons transplanted here by Charlemagne.[1] They built their fortress where a Roman castle had stood, and they bred a fierce race of warriors. Many are the tales people will tell you of the place. Let one suffice.

I walked out in the dusk one night to the ruins from Müllerthal with a young man of the village for company. The owls were particularly noisy.

" Griselinda's voice ! " remarked my companion. " Do you hear it ? "

" What ? The noise of the owls ? "

" Yes."

[1] See p. 26 .

" And thereby hangs a tale, doubtless "—and there does.

If Heringerburg was famous for its fierce warriors, no less renowned was it for its fair ladies, and of the castle's " Dream of Fair Women " the most beautiful was Griselinda. She was known far and wide for the exquisite beauty of her voice, clear as the nightingale. There were evidently musical critics in those days, but Griselinda was protected against them by a power which, doubtless, more than one singer since would have given much to possess. Did any one venture to deny her supremacy in vocal art, that person was immediately turned to stone. To live, every one had to pay homage to her gift of song. " And these rocks," said my companion, " are the overbold critics," whose daring has certainly given them a stability not shared by the dust of those who heard and admired. As the evening shadows lengthened, the fair Griselinda would stand by her window—was it that which can still be seen in the single wall that remains standing? She had a habit which even to-day singers suburban have not cured themselves of. She sang at an open window ; all the vale heard the glorious liquid notes ; she—

> Made
> *Her* music heard below.

And of admirers she had indeed a goodly tally. There were some whose admiration just saved them from petrifaction, and from that point there was a crescendo of adoration which reached its highest in the heart of the young and handsome lord of Folken-

dange, who doubtless was seigneur of a neighbouring
castle, though exactly where it stood I know not.

One evening the fair songstress was in more than
usually good voice, and the music had such an effect
that the young nobleman could no longer resist the
temptation to tell the beautiful one of his love.
Evidently the lord of Heringerburg was at home,
for the young lover did not dare to go to the
castle by way of the main entrance. He set out to
climb the rock straight up to the window of this
local Lorelei. He had almost succeeded in his effort,
when he became so greatly entranced by a part of
Griselinda's song that he forgot to hold on. Down
he fell to the foot of the rock, more than a hundred
yards below.

Griselinda rushed from the castle height—by the
proper way, wisely !—and found the young lord of
Folkendange dead. Then she sang her last song,
the most plaintive of all her melodies. Some months
afterwards she died, but still her notes are heard
in the woodbine, and you can say that those of the
owl are hers without great danger of being turned
to stone.

A little below Vögelsmühle the Hallerbach runs
into the Erenz Noire, and by a path a few hundred
yards farther on we turn aside to explore this
beautiful little vale. No other that I have seen is so
rich in flower and fern—flowers of all the hues from
pale blue to deepest scarlet, ferns of all kinds to
the fairest and gentlest maidenhair that ever grew.
And what glorious tapestry the varicoloured mosses
have woven underfoot and on the rocks which do

not trouble the clear, easy-going stream ! Then,
after a wander of—well, it may be one mile, it may
be twenty, the Nature lover will have no idea, nor
wish to have, of the length of the Hallerbach from
the Müllerthal to where he leaves it at the point where
Taupeschbach (or Hubertusbach) relieves the Hallerbach as guide to Beaufort. As for the Hallerbach
itself, it attempts no startling effects. At times it
enjoys a cascade, but mostly it dallies in pools across
which the trout flash like arrows from the bow,
Here and there it will spread its scant waters out
so as to make little islands.

.Where the two streams join, the picture is one of
the most exquisite beauty. On the left a huge rocky
keep stands guard ; on the right the valley wall falls
sharply. Right up to the point where you leave the
woodland and see Beaufort castle, the entrancing
charm of the vale is preserved. Here, you cannot
help thinking, is a path which will make the wanderer
disregard one of the first rules of wandering and
return by the same way.

The valley leads you to the southern side of
Beaufort village, just to the spot where stands
another castle of renown. It is a magnificent coup
d'œil which greets one on emerging from the woods.
Right in front, barring the valley, stands a gigantic
ruin, the old castle towering proudly on high, well
preserved, still keeping the nobility and the elegance
which the Renaissance gave it. The slender towers,
the long, mullioned windows, give it a grace few
other old castles in the Grand Duchy possess. Beside
it stands the new castle, of the seventeenth century,

11

a charming construction flanked by a square tower roofed with slates, and with a great court faced by arcade-like buildings.

It is not possible to put an exact date to the old castle, but very old it is. The lords of Beaufort, or Befort, as it was then, were a branch of the tree of the Wiltz nobility. As early as 1236 they were busy in Luxembourg history, and a Befort seigneur appended his signature to the famous " charte d'affranchissement " which Ermesinde awarded the bourgeoisie of Echternach.

In 1593 the Lord of Beaufort, Gaspard de Heu, placed his sword and strength at the disposal of the Orange party, and Philip II, an Alva of an earlier age, wrought vengeance on that castle, as well as on Vianden, for the temerity of its overlord. And the overlord he promptly beheaded. Philip made a gift of the castle to his favourite, Mansfeld.

Fifty years after, Beaufort became associated with one of the most romantic of Luxembourg's heroes— Jean Beck. Beck began life as a herd-boy, and rose to the position eventually of Governor of Luxembourg. He became a soldier of fortune in the Austrian army, and his discovery of a conspiracy against the ruling house not only put his feet upon the ladder of advancement but sent him up its steps at a pace which might have turned any one's head. In his soldier's knapsack he found a field-marshal's baton. He is chiefly remembered in the Grand Duchy for his exploits in the Thirty Years War, deeds which make him one of Luxembourg's darling heroes.

BEAUFORT CASTLE.

A curious and interesting story is told of him as showing how his suddenly acquired fame did not make him proud. When yet a poor young fellow he married a slattern market girl whose way compelled him to part from her. Yet when, as Governor, he entered Luxembourg in pomp, he had not forgotten her ; he had searched her out, and by his side she shared the homage and honour paid to him by the city.

With place came naturally riches, and he was able to acquire the castle of Beaufort for the sum of 60,000 florins. He used it as barracks, and he it was who erected the new castle. Beck died at Arras in 1648, refusing to allow any one to bind the wounds which he received at the battle of Lens. After his death the old castle was abandoned and fell gradually into ruins. In 1817 the Count de Liedekerke-Beaufort acquired it, and hastened the process of ruin by taking some of the materials to erect a mill, and he offered no objection to the villagers helping themselves to material for repairing cottages and doing other mason's work. In that way the principal tower disappeared. In time, however, that vandalism was happily put a stop to. The modern castle belongs to M. Linckels, who uses part of the old edifice as a " fabrique de conserves " which produces a " Kirschwasser " esteemed above that of the Black Forest, and greatly appreciated by artists who make of Beaufort another Pont Aven.

And Beaufort is certainly an artistic little place. Its houses are old and not always perpendicular ; some of the streets are flights of stairs, and there is at least one good, very good, inn, whose host is the worthy M. Bleser.

From pretty little Beaufort a malle-post runs to Reisdorf, through pretty country, twice a day ; but before we leave the Müllerthal region let me quote this description of it from the pen of Goerres, disciple of Schelling, as given by M. Jean d'Ardenne from the *Reinische Merkur*:—

"La contrée est d'une beauté particulière et comparable à l'antique séjour des géants. Des rocs dénudés, émergeant du sol et des forêts qui ont grandi autour d'eux, font des couronnements aux crêtes des deux rives, dont ils suivent toutes les sinuosités. Leurs formes aux arêtes vives, leurs assises colossales, leur donnent l'aspect de réelles forteresses titaniques, dont les murs et les tours se seraient enfouis peu à peu sous le sol, ne montrant plus que leurs amortissements crénelés entre les frondaisons de la forêt vierge. Et il semble que les hôtes de ces châteaux gigantesques, isolés chacun sur sa cime, se soient livrés entre eux, en un jour de colère fol, un combat acharné. Du haut en bas des versant et jusque dans le lit de la rivière, des blocs énormes se rencontrent, comme si on les avait lancés et roulés, et ils donnent vraiment l'image exact du combat des Titans. Dans le Müllerthal, surtout, l'action parait avoir été très vive. Mais tant d'années ont passé là-dessus que la nature a repris tous ses droits, revêtant les rochers de mousse et de lierre et faisant surgir de leurs crevasses des arbres aux puissantes ramures."

With that short description, an interlude from a

pen usually dipped in gall for political propaganda, we leave the Millers' Dale with many a delightful memory and the hope that one day we may tread again its lovely ways.

ACROSS COUNTRY TO MERSCH

Voices out of the shade that cried,
And long noon in the hot calm places,
And children's play by the wayside,
And country eyes, and quiet faces—
All these were round my steady paces.

RUPERT BROOKE.

CHAPTER VI

ACROSS COUNTRY TO MERSCH

THE ways by which the wanderer may leave Echternach appear to be inexhaustible. They all lead
into the woodlands which encircle the town from river
to river, but that which leads up into the Forest of
Hardt is one of the most charming. The Forest of
Hardt is by far the most extensive of the forests
on the right bank of the Sure, and there is a pathway
leading right through the deeps of its green heart.
So by that way we shall start our cross-country
wander.

The road to take is that which branches off to the
left just opposite the Hotel Bellevue. It is a pleasant,
rural Unter den Linden leading along the Kappellen-
bach. Straight ahead it goes for nearly a mile,
and then, at the outskirts of the forest, river and
road part company, and a steep path tempts the
wanderer into the woodland shade. For about an
hour and a half you have a forest footpath all to
yourself. There is no mistaking it. Moss-grown
boulders, the loveliest of ferns, flowers in plenty,
the bluebells and heather of this southern Scotland,
a ribbon of a pathway " alluring up and enticing
down "—all these go to make the mise-en-scène.

Far too soon the farmyard sounds of Michelshof will tell that the end of that part of the journey is reached.

At Michelshof five roads meet, or, counting the Hardt pathway, six. To the right, about a mile and a half away over fields and woods, lies Scheidgen ; but there is a roundabout way, for those who have time, which is much more interesting than the direct route. About half-way, farmlands give way to the woods which clothe the Rosswinkel height. Then on the right a pathway cuts up into the forest, and soon the invader will hear the music of two streams which rise on the wooded slope and join together to sport down the rocky gallery called Ponteschgrund. Not all the explorations recorded in the last chapter have exhausted the toll of the attractions of this picturesque borderland, and the narrow way of the Ponteschgrund, hemmed in by trees, decked by Flora, cut by a singing rivulet and with rocks thrown about in most fascinating disorder, is one of the longest in the district. It takes a good half-hour to pass through this gorge where the gods rioted. At the end is Scheidgen once more —a village loosely scattered along the Echternach-Consdorf road and that from Michelshof. Scheidgen's railway station stands some little way distant, as is often the case with station and village in this part of the country. And the name given to the stopping-places varies curiously. Echternach, of course, has a full-blown " gare " ; Consdorf lays claim to a " station " ; while the inhabitant of Scheidgen, wishing to travel, goes to the " halte."

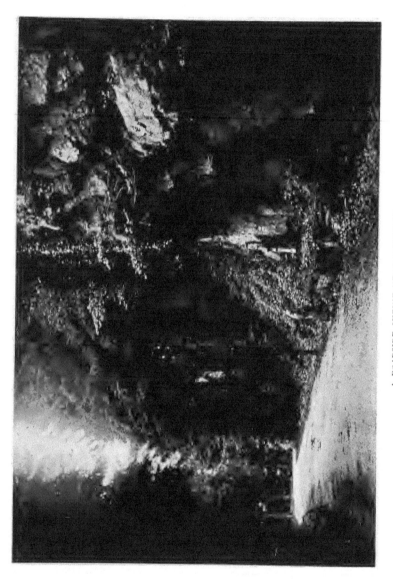

A ROADSIDE SHRINE NEAR CONSDORF.

We have now reached the delightful "route de Consdorf," and along it the village of the name is quickly reached. It is a most straggling place, spreading from the railway station for about a mile along a maze of intersecting roads. Usually for visitors to the Müllerthal region it is the centre, and that is just why I have led you through the little Switzerland of Luxembourg without visiting the village. It will be seen at a glance that Consdorf looks for a good few people to come its way. At least I counted no fewer than ten inns and cafés. Nine seem to have exhausted all the names the dear, simple villagers could think of, and with the tenth they had to start using them over again. An obliging wayfarer had recommended the "Nussbaum" to me as a place of refreshment, and when, in the village, I inquired where it was, I was asked which of the two "Nut Trees" I particularly desired ! More years ago than I care to count I first became acquainted with Consdorf, and it is curious, after a space of time, to visit such little lost villages again and to note the complete absence of the spirit of change. Custom holds progress at bay ; everything is tried by the low standard of use ; things that will do need not be altered—that is the village philosophy of life.

The road from Consdorf to the south is a good one and pleasant—the same route which, coming from Berdorf, manages to extricate itself in good order from the confusion of Consdorf, and which leads, by field and forest, to Alttrier. But there is a more interesting way to reach that castra hiberna of the Romans. About five hundred yards down the hill from the station a sign-post indicates the presence of a pathway, and that will be found to lead along the Consdorferbach valley ; and, seeing that the little stream rises but a short distance from Alttrier, it as well as the road may be taken as guide. In my opinion a river is always preferable to a road. A road is a happy enough companion, being generally without history, but a river is history from the beginning. A road is often an intruder in a scene ; but the river was there before man began to make history, and without it there would be no history and no scenery. So up the Consdorferbach we shall go—a delightfully attractive wander— until we reach the little village of Hersberg, where the bach is born. And Alttrier is not far away.

It may be well for the wanderer to know that Alttrier is not recognized locally—at least, so I found. The place is called Shanz—simplicity again, for that, being interpreted, is " intrenchment " or " bulwark." And that is what the Romans made of Alttrier's height, a fine spacious plateau to which the glints of Echternach's spires come across the intervening seas of green. Alttrier was the right of the line of important camps which the Romans made facing the forests they had reason to fear. Until a date within memory no one worried to penetrate the covering Time and the elements had thrown over the place upon which the camp stood, but when the exploring spade set to work numerous coins, vases, jewels and inscriptions were unearthed, the latter telling sufficient to give ground for the belief that

the camp was laid out in the reign of the Emperor
Arcadius. When road-making here in 1844 an altar
to Jupiter was unearthed. It is of red sandstone, and
has the inscription : " Deo optimo maximo ara
dedicata." [1] This treasure is to be seen in the
museum at Luxembourg.

Rome has left much to tell her story in this part
of the Grand Duchy. And here the worst of it is
that there is no proper road, and that no guide-book,
sign-post or native can tell you the way from Alttrier
to Christnach. And that was undoubtedly the reason
why I chose Christnach as my next stopping-place.
But if you have the bump of locality and direction,
then set off north-west, roughly, by any path you
chance to find leading from the north side of the
Alttrier road. And let wanderers be warned ; let
them be up with the sun to take the road. Through
woods, across fields, past, here and there, tiny villages
surrounded by fruit-trees, about four kilometres will
bring the tramp to the valley of the Black Erenz,
probably, if he keeps well to the north, via Breitweiler. A Roman road used to lead from this village
to Medernach, north of Fels, and many Roman relics
have been found. The bridge near by across the
river marks the southern end of the Müllerthal, and
upstream for four or five miles stretches a vale
worthy indeed of its name—Blumenthal. Of that,
however, I shall have something to say later. But
before leaving Breitweiler the St. Hubert Chapel
should be visited. It stands where stood a little

[1] " The altar is consecrated to the god supreme "—Jupiter,
under his title "Optimus Maximus."

temple built when the Romans were in the neighbourhood, and much of the old material was used to build the modern edifice. The most interesting part of what has survived is the altar, among the carvings of which is a figure of the cruel goddess Mania. Across the bridge, and on the way to Christnach, there appears on the right of the route to Wolfsberg, or Wolfsfelt, a gentle slope, upon which stand the ruins of a temple of old. It must date from about the same period as that of St. Quirinus, beside the Petrusse in Luxembourg ; and, indeed, second-century coins have been found beside it. An arched and columned porch leads into what was the interior of the temple, and part of it was cut out of the solid rock. Many people, and the inscription as well, suggest that the building was a villa and not a temple, but I think it is much more likely to have been a place of worship. It was used for four centuries before the overthrow of Rome. And its builders " builded better than they knew," for, as the inscription says, nearly seventeen centuries leave a very considerable portion of it standing. Of course, there is the usual inscription. It is a curious thing that when the Luxembourger puts up a plaque he cannot resist composing a puzzle for it. That on the Hollay rock is an example, and here is another. The inscription is in German, in small and large capitals, and if the large letters are added together as Roman numerals the date of the setting up of the inscription will be discovered. Seeing, however, that the letters make this array—

ICIIIVILLDIIIVLVVDIIIVIVDIIVVVIIIIL,

most people, however strong in mental arithmetic, will at once take my word for it that the carved stone received its inscription in the year 1863. And I took some one else's word for it !

Many of the Roman relics have been gathered together at a mill near by—Ölsmühle, or, if you need to inquire for it from a native, Oligsmühle. It was the birthplace of the Abbé Engling, who, with his brother, took great interest in the discovery and collection of relics of Roman times. It was the brother who discovered the Wolfsberg remains in 1844. The mill is a curious place. The art of the Roman decks it ; sculptured stones, heads, coins and all kinds of relics are there ; and in the adjoining garden what could not be housed are set out in picturesque array with many kinds of flowers around. I had a long chat with the jolly miller, and one thing surprised me. I shall put it in this form : I hope no American will ever go that way, because I am sure he would obtain many interesting relics for little trouble and at less cost. I did not buy, though I might, I believe, have done so ; for I had no desire to be counted, even though the counting might be secret, among those who helped to despoil the work of the good Abbé Engling or to rob Luxembourg of the smallest of her relics.

Christnach, another of those wide-straggling, cross-road villages so common in the Grand Duchy, is a sign of Rome and of the Cross. Rome built it ; the Cross changed it, faith and name. It was originally Crucenacum, and, centuries after, Crucenach for short. Here was a temple to Diana, upon the stones of which the church of to-day rests, though more than one edifice has stood there since the pagan fane of old fell to ruins. And so it is with a surprisingly large number of the houses of the village. In their walls still remain the stones which Roman hands cut and carved. Yet a sad enough little place it is—poor, and picturesque only in patches, though with a delightful background of hill and beech forests. Fels is only three miles away as the crow flies, but farther away by our route, so as the wanderer has come far, and must spend the next day at Fels, let him wend his way to the Hotel Koch, where fare is simple, accommodation happily clean if limited, and people talkative when twilight descends and drives them indoors to the light and company of the inn parlour.

And how did Crucenach become Christnach? It was not by any mutilation of name, near though the two be to each other in sound and appearance. For the change is a landmark in local history, dating from some period only vaguely determined as being six hundred and something, probably very nearly seven hundred, when from Trier and Echternach the Church was spreading its warriors of the .Word abroad through the lands. Up those beautiful vales of the Black Erenz came the gospel-bearers, prosecuting their mission amid constant dangers and difficulties among the people who had ousted Rome and who worshipped the gods of Gaul. Lord of a great extent of country was Rodoric, or Rodoricus, whose writ ran far around from his fastness on the Rock of Fels. Three miles through the forest lived

a noble Germanic family, one of whom was Schwanhilde, who had been converted to Christianity by
the missionaries from Trier.   Rodoric loved her,
but she would have nothing to do with him till he
forsook his gods of stone and wood and pagan
imagination.   It followed as a natural result that the
determined maiden was cast into prison.   Every day
for a year the pagan lord of Fels came to her
dungeon to offer her freedom and his hand if she
would abandon this new, strange faith.   But no ; she
would only yield if he would overthrow the Temple
to Diana, slaughter with the axe the trees of the
dark, forbidding grove around it, and, unhid upon
the height, rear a temple to her God.   One day
Rodoric found the dungeon empty and his captive
gone.   The haughty chief swore that his gods had
dealt ill with him and that the God of Schwanhilde
had beaten them.   So it was with crumbling faith, dis-
consolately rather than with anger, that he searched
for the missing fair one, and as the old gods had
not helped him to success he was all the more
willing to listen to the gospel of the Trierian monks.
In the end Rodoric bowed to the Cross, and swore
he would do as Schwanhilde had required of him.
And the maiden had not fled far away.   In a cave
within sight of the castle she had waited and watched
and prayed.   The monks brought her word of the
conversion of the lord of Fels, and she went forth
to meet him.   Before the axe of his retainers Diana's
grove fell ; the temple was overthrown, and a little
Christian church quickly took its place.   In it Rodoric
and Schwanhilde were married.   In token of her

12

gladness and thanks she changed her name to Christina, and the little town that lifted its eyes to the hill upon which the new temple stood became Christnach, or Christina's town.

But Celt has left his mark as well as Roman. Let us take a roundabout way to Fels. It is via Graulinster, Junglinster, Burgelinster and Altlinster, all four lying scattered in valleys of Black and White Erenz. We return to Breitweiler bridge and ascend the Blumenthal, through which the Black Erenz sings, woefully misnamed, though tribute in name denied to the river has been bestowed upon the valley. For it is a valley of flowers, this rugged river vale ; its rocks are thrown high and low ; they make the river sing the merriest of songs of companionship as its waters kiss the rough anger of stones into the smoothness of friendship. Mosses grow down to listen and to drink ; flowers bend their lovely heads and, with colour's melodious voice of praise, join in Nature's hymn. Unspoilt Nature is like a dim and venerable fane : it commands a heart's tribute. So by a ribbon-like pathway, fallen at random where there was room, a light tracing of footsteps which have scarcely worn a zigzag way over the forest's carpet, the wanderer goes, until Graulinster calls from the left across the stream. And why all those " linsters "? It was the Celt who threw a handful of them down by the two rivers. " Ster " means a river and " lin " a marsh, and the name Linster became that of one of the most important domains of all old Luxembourg. The lords of Linster had their feudal stronghold at Burgelinster, and in the

BURGELINSTER.

history of the Duchy their doings are not surpassed
in number and their power in importance by those
of any other house in the land.   It was not by war
but by the claims of succession that their power was
broken ; the domain was divided and the divisions
were subdivided ; there was, for once in a way,
no power in numbers.   At Burgelinster, between
the old and the young Linsters and the two rivers,
two towers and some ruins of their castle are to be
seen ; the last branch upon a stupendous family
tree withered only towards the end of last century.
Here the two rivers almost meet, little more than
half a mile separating them.   Typical villages are
the four Linsters, set down in charming country.

Junglinster church is well worth a visit.   Built,
in Renaissance style, in the second half of the
eighteenth century, it suffered, with others, from the
outrages of the Revolution, but it has been tastefully
restored.   The frescoes in the choir are the work of
Echternach monks.   The vault of the choir carries
a beautiful Majestas Domini—Christ, on a throne of
cloud, surrounded by angels, the patriarchs, the
prophets, the saints of the Old and New Testa-
ment.   Below, on the earth, the seven cardinal
virtues are seen personified, and at the four corners
are the four saintly Fathers of the Church.   The
high altar and the pulpit are magnificent pieces of
carved work, as are the confessional boxes, the
communion bench, the organ and the rood-loft.

Altminster we visit last, because it is on the White
Erenz, which is our pathway to Fels.   The tiny
village has no more than a hundred and eighty

inhabitants, though one would think that its ideal
position by the river and the richness of its surroundings would attract many more people to it. But the
straggling place has its one " sight." This is scarcely
to be found without guidance, but there are many
small guides to be found in Altminster's straggling
" streets." The " sight " is an old piece of Celtic
carving to be found among the neighbouring white
rocks which give the name of the river its adjective.
It is the Herthesley, or Rock of Hertha. Two
thousand years old it is, the little guide will say—
a romantically long period to him. On the face of
the rock is a huge piece of relief carving, twelve
feet or so high and eight broad. It is as though
some mighty die had left its imprint on the rock.
There are two huge figures of a man and a woman,
and no older trace of man's work is to be found in
the country. It looks as though the woman were
veiled. But the storms of two thousand years or
more have played sad havoc with detail : the man's
head has disappeared altogether. So indistinct is
the whole thing that some people are of opinion
that it is the female figure that is headless. And as
to the identity of the pair, beliefs vary too. Hertha,
or Erda, Earth-goddess, " prophetess of things
eternal," and Mannus,[1] some say they are ; to others
the man is but the priest of Hertha ; others say it
is merely a tomb-carving. Yet another belief is that
the two figures represent a couple of slaves in the
gladiators' prison, waiting to enter the arena either

---

[1] " The first man," son of the god Tuisco, forefather of the
Istaevones, the Ingaevones and the Herminones.

to fight with or to be devoured by wild animals. That, however, is hard to believe. I hold to the opinion that the Celtic Ung who carved it carved Hertha and her priest. Names near at hand are all Celtic. There is, close by, Freyley, or Freystein (Frëia's Rock), and a neighbouring cavern is Hertegeswey, the same divinity's armoury. And it is believed that the top of the Herthesley was an altar for Druid sacrifice ; there are still traces of steps to the top. There a magnificent view can be obtained. All the Linsters are visible and both rivers—a wide stretch of greenery and gold and silver, with a drab element introduced by the villages. It is a very great pity that precautions have not been taken to protect this relic against wind and rain and sun. Long ago would it have been obliterated were it not that the rock has fallen a little forward, thus protecting the carved part. It is a curious piece of work, which could never have been anything else but rough and uncouth—one of man's earliest scribbles in his nursery.

> Changed are the Gods of Hunt and Dance,
> And he with these.

But not " Farewell, Romance ! " That still lives through all changes, whether of growth or decay. Locally the " sight " is called De Man and Fra op der Lé.

Most people arrive in Fels by the miniature railway which comes from the main Luxembourg-Ettelbrück line at Kruchten. It must be the smallest public railway in use in the world, I should think.

The engines are little toy things and move at a
sedate pace, taking a solid five minutes for each
mile of the eight between the two towns. Though
a whole carriage, generally in two compartments,
does not carry more than a score of people, they
are very comfortable. There are no stations en route,
but the train stops occasionally at places marked
out for stopping by a " café de la gare " and a
" boîte aux lettres," and the guard descends to inspect
both in search of animate and inanimate loads. The
station building at Fels, right up in the town by
the church, is more like a London cabman's shelter
than anything else that I can think of.

It is in the centre of a long and wide " place "
that the railway line comes to an end. You see at
once that Fels (in French, La Rochette) has a great
weakness for trees. They are everywhere ; trees
to the native constitute the whole art of natural
decoration. The market-place is thickly planted with
lindens, and, truth to tell, Berlin might well envy
some of them and covet them for her famous
thoroughfare. Beech and pine and fir thickly clothe
all the surrounding heights, and the proud inhabitants
are very anxious that they should be admired. And
admiration is most certainly their due, though beautiful work could be done with shrubs and flowers
in the height-encircled market-place. Then, again,
the fine old castle is hidden away in trees, and, if
you are a photographer, it means a hard climb on
the opposite height to get a picture which will show
much of the ruins of the venerable citadel.

The town is closely packed by the White Erenz

and between the " massifs " which give it its descriptive name. Here the angler may bring out his rod, for up and down stream fish are fairly plentiful. Though not so far away from the middle of things, though attracting by its beauty a goodly number of holiday-makers, Fels is strangely out of the world, curiously childish in modern things. About world-happenings the people are quite content to remain in ignorance. In one little hotel there last autumn (1912) I found a score of people in a sitting-room having an afternoon chat. Not one of them had heard as much as a word of the foundering of the *Titanic*. Only one knew that the North Pole had been discovered, and thought the matter of no importance ! Those who candidly confessed they did not know said that they had forgotten the name of the French President. The people have one amusement, and that is provided four times daily. It is the arrival and departure of the train. Their interest in that never flags, winter or summer. They are not even very interested in their own surroundings—historical or geographical. I wonder what the village schoolmaster is about ! However, I did discover one exception to the rule. In a market-place hotel I was greeted by mine host with the words, " My daughter will be glad to see you." The young lady appeared, and we had an interesting chat—in English. Mademoiselle, I discovered, read the *Daily Telegraph* carefully every day !

Fels first appears in history as an important stronghold, about the time of William the Norman. A place with such fine natural claims was bound to be chosen as somebody's stronghold, and the possessor of it was just as certain to become a powerful personage. And mighty rulers the lords of Fels were for long ages, making history in camp and at court ; from the Crusades to the Revolution there was not much that happened in which lords of Fels had not some share. It was the redoubtable Marshal Boufflers who brought ruin upon their magnificent castle in his long and fairly thorough campaign against the strongholds of the Duchy. Neglected and in ruins it lay, until in 1840 it was bought by the Grand Duke, who took steps to preserve what was left.

It is a marvel of militant masonry, reached nowadays by a stairway up the wooded height. You will find the gateway barred and an instruction to ring the bell. And it is necessary to ring loudly, for the guardian has a large domain to look after and the sound of the bell may have to carry a long way. What was evidently the courtyard of the castle is now laid out as a sort of park, trees clustering as thickly as they do outside the walls. Everything is " in order." There are benches at shady spots, well-kept paths ; Monsieur le gardien has seen to it that there is no danger of your falling down the rock if you happen to become enthusiastic about a certain view ; the bounds of terra firma are clearly and strongly set. And from this part of the height there are certainly many glorious views to be had over hill and forest and town. Scattered about this novel park are odds and ends of ruins, and behind it lies the cluster of the remains of the donjon. They are fairly well preserved. A number of rooms may be visited after admiring the façade, which in all its glory must have been exquisite, and is still fine. High up, like an inaccessible niche in the wall, is a pointed apse with its beautiful little columns and its tasteful carvings. Here was the castle chapel in days of old.

I wonder Fels does not have nightmare on windy nights, for it must have noticed that this huge wall would work enormous damage on the town below were it to fall. Fels evidently has faith in the builders of long ago, and perhaps it is warranted. There are a score of places in Luxembourg where castle walls should fall and bury houses and people. But they don't. They were master builders who reared them. If they were modern walls, I scarcely think people would " sleep peacefully in their beds " below them. Inside the donjon is the castle well, about 180 feet deep. It was famous in its early days for the cold and crystal-clear water which was drawn from the rocky deep. But as lovesick maidens threw themselves into it, as desperate warriors preferred death by water to an end by steel, as babies whom some one thought de trop were consigned on dark nights to its depths, and as money, plate and various treasures were sunk there in times of danger, it is little wonder—for all such things happened— that the supply of water deteriorated in quality and became a byword. But, in these calmer and less exciting days, it has had time to recover. The castle-rock dragon which waits for toothsome tribute at the bottom of the well has lean years now.

Not far away the guardian and his wife have their abode, and the extent of the plateau may be gauged from the fact that, in addition to the extensive park and ruins mentioned, they have room for a good-sized farmyard. Behind is the main entrance to the castle, arched, with two round towers and with a fixed bridge in place of the ancient drawbridge over the fosse. Here we leave the castle, and the guide's last act is to unlock a curious little cupboard in which he keeps the visitors' book. I generally turn my back on such volumes, but the guardian begged me to sign, "as no Englishman had visited the castle for a long time."

" And," I added, " no legible writer for much longer."

,Why is it, I wonder, that those who write their names in visitors' books almost invariably provide a Chinese puzzle with every entry?

And skirting a wood, then cutting through and descending by narrow paths, one leaves the historic height. There is such a maze of paths that one is almost certain to take the wrong one and reach the road after incursions into the backyards and gardens of the houses that face it. But in Luxembourg, as a fairly general rule, you may go wherever a gate opens.

Through all the wooded heights around the town there are pleasant walks, with a " belvedere " at every possible point and a seat after every climb. On the height opposite the castle an old watch-tower stands, and from that point can be seen what trees and climbing ivy and creeping moss prevent

IFLS CASTLE.

closer at hand—the magnificently large extent of the castle domain, and one can conjure up in one's mind what a defiant fortress it once had been.

Fels has about 1,300 inhabitants, and one out of every two nearly is employed in cloth-weaving. That is the one thing in which the village has shown enterprise, and it has been rewarded by good trade and the importance of being one of the most important centres of that particular industry in the Duchy.

Next to Fels the most important place in the district in the feudal ages was Meysembourg, a little more than three miles away. Early in the twelfth century a formidable castle stood there, and for two hundred years the barons held by no means a little world in awe. Then the fighting stock died out and another race took possession. A quarrelsome lot they appear to have been, for Meysembourg, history tells us, was constantly being besieged. As the result of one " little war," about the end of the sixteenth century, it was completely destroyed. Rebuilt, it had about a century's comparative peace, until, in 1684, that great warrior Marshal Boufflers came along, and, not content with half-measures in this case as in most others, he razed it to the ground. Before the French Revolution Baron Christophe d'Arnoult put up a modern little palace, and from him it passed to his son-in-law, the Comte de Wiltz. The count fled before the Revolutionaries, who seized his possessions and knocked them down to the highest bidder. That person was " Monsieur Antoine, Baron de Casal de Fischbach," the absurd

sum of 900,000 francs being fixed upon. But as
the amount was payable in paper money, perhaps
" Monsieur Antoine's " banking account was not de-
pleted to that extent.   The place changed hands
again before it came into the hands of the present
owners, the d'Arenberg family, who have improved
it very considerably.   Prince Charles d'Arenberg,
the first of the family to enjoy this lovely retreat,
married Julia, Countess Hunyady, the widow of the
vigorous Prince Michael Obrenovitch III of Servia,
who was assassinated on June 10, 1868.

Meysembourg Castle, looking modern, rising high
with its two large turrets and a cluster of small
ones, standing amid beautiful trees, sheltered and
peaceful near a little river and a lovely lake, suggests
nothing of the history of the place.   Not a remnant
of feudal times remains.   All castles of the Middle
Ages drew round them a village of retainers, and
so did Meysembourg.   But even that has vanished
without leaving a trace.   The villagers, aggravated
by the cruel treatment and harsh laws of " Monsieur
Antoine," left the neighbourhood, and that Revolutionary aristocrat, another Rufus, cleared their houses
out of the way to add to the dimensions of his
grounds.

Six kilometres from Meysembourg, by a charming road through the wooded ravine of the Rol-
linsgerbach, and Mersch in its wide and fertile plain
is reached.

Mersch was Maresca up to the ninth century,
then Maresch, from which the transition to the name
of to-day was not long in coming.   Marsh, of course,

it means. Geologists tell us that the sea once swept
up Luxembourg, leaving Vianden's rock a little islet
some way from the shore. At a time to which no
record save that of Mother Earth goes back the
sea gradually receded, and when the earliest inhabitants were busy devising names for the places
where they lived and hunted and fished and fought,
they lived on a marsh land. Hence Mersch and
the " lin " of the four Linsters. But the marshes
have gone, and a far-spreading and fertile prairie,
decked with woods, its rivers heralded in outline
from afar by rows of trees, spreads from Mersch to
Junglinster.

I have reached Mersch from north and south and
west by road and rail ; I have come to it, guided
by its towers, from all those directions, fishing-rod in
hand ; I have tramped into it from the woods of
the east. Three rivers and six roads lead to it,
so there is no escape. There is a curious charm
about the place, with its one long, straggling street
between Eisch and Mamer, and the rest of it thrown
down anywhere and anyhow. There is charm to
please, vandalism to make you angry, and charm
again to soothe away your wrath.

I have never agreed with Robert Louis Stevenson about the tragedy of arrival at a place which
one has looked forward to seeing. Some places disappoint, it may be bitterly, but there is, to my mind,
always something about every place which prevents
the tragedy of disappointment if one brings to it
the right spirit of appreciation, which means im-
bibing something of the patriotism of place. With-

out that I can imagine myself painting Mersch as a tragedy. But let me see how I do paint it !

Vis-à-vis de la gare, as the guide-books say, a quaint old hostelry welcomes the visitor—the " Brandenburger." There the guest still has his expenditure chalked up on a huge slate. He dines by candle-light. Stairs and floors creak with age. And I know no more charming, inn in Luxembourg's length and breadth, no more genial hostess than Madame of the " Brandenburger." She makes the traveller at home at once, and her presence turns the company in the café into a happy family. The birds of passage and the local worthies are soon on the very best of terms. Mersch was one of the first places I ever visited in the Grand Duchy ; its story was first told me in the Brandenburger café in dialect of the broadest, with which I was then only so slightly familiar that in endeavouring to follow it I felt like a very young schoolboy attempting to decipher the last intricacies—if, indeed, such intricacies are not like Tennyson's brook—of algebra.

Mersch has two curiosities ; they stand at the opposite end of the town from the station, and can be seen from far and wide in the neighbourhood. One is a tall tower, capped with a black Eastern cupola. Here is the visitor's first disappointment. Surely a fine old church stands with the tower. But no ! The tower stands lonely and by itself in a large square ; the church—for there was one up to a little more than sixty years ago—has disappeared. And a magnificent, interesting, historical edifice it was, and one of the finest of the ancient

buildings in the whole of the country. Roman, Gaul
and Frank had contributed their quota to it, and,
indeed, relics of that trio of conquering and con-
quered races are still found thickly scattered over
Mersch's plain. In 1851, however, the powers that
were decided on the demolition of the church, and
carried their design into all too hurried execution.
But the Queen-Mother of Holland heard of the work
of destruction. Her Majesty was of the Imperial
House of Russia, and the Oriental tower, which she
had seen several times, recalled to her mind the
towers of Moscow and of her native land. So she
expressed the wish that it might be saved from the
hands of the destroyers. The royal wish was obeyed,
and that is how the curious, odd erection remains,
saved for a Western land by the Eastern style of
its architect. Some of the salvage from the
wreck, mostly carvings, is to be seen in Luxembourg Museum. They would have been so infinitely
better where they were. A little farther along the
street stands the new church, a huge, ungainly building, without any of the distinction of art in its
making. Its front looks, indeed, more like that
of a theatre than a church. In truth, Luxembourg
has not been very successful with its modern churches,
but that at Mersch exceeds all in ugliness ; it is
the last word in huge crudity.

Near the tower is the ancient château fort of
Mersch. The building, now a farmhouse, is a dull-
looking place from the outside, standing high and
gaunt, still surrounded by its ancient ditches. And
for some reason unknown to taste or necessity this

old castle and its gateway have been splashed over with light red paint, making the place an eyesore, a grotesque daub of crude colour in the landscape.

The feudal lords of Mersch were as much renowned for their enlightened rule as for their fighting bravery, and in both their fame lasted long. It was one of Mersch's long roll of brave men who, at the time of the Princess Ermesinde, founded the Convent of Marienthal, which we shall visit in the next chapter.

On the gate is to be seen the coat-of-arms of John Frederick of Autel, last of his line, who died in 1716. He was a general in the army, Governor of Luxembourg and Chevalier of the Golden Fleece. It was towards the end of the sixteenth century that the castle was restored and added to as we see it to-day, and certainly the old style of things preserved in the interior compensates for the exterior ugliness. Beautiful apartments are found in the rez-de-chaussée and on the first floor, one of the first-floor vaulted rooms being a particularly fine one. The original stone staircase is still preserved. The castle has indeed been fortunate. Boufflers, destroyer-in-chief in Luxembourg, had no reason to turn his cannon upon it, for it bade him no defiance.

That exhausts Mersch as far as curiosities are concerned. Alone they would rightly disappoint those who had imagined that the little town (it has three thousand inhabitants), lying where three river valleys meet, right in the heart of the country, must be a much more interesting place. But what Mersch fails to provide in historical remains and however

much it has mishandled what it has and had, it
compensates for everything by means of its most
delightful position. Its great plain of rolling green,
its woods and distant hills, a glorious home of

The mighty choric god,
The great hill-haunting and tree-loving Pan,

and above all the three charming rivers at its doors
—these are what call the wanderer to Mersch ; these
are beauty enough.

Of Eisch and Mamer the next chapter will tell,
but before the call of other scenes is responded to
let us wander down the Alzette for a little. Different
it is from the small stream we saw among the
towering crags of the capital and left, framed in
beauty, at Hesperange. It has grown by the tribute
which others have poured into it ; it is now a
lovely tingling flood of mystic pearl, a string of
opals with veins full of quivering light. To the
artist in the sunny days its beauty is a delight, and
the angler will find that it is better to fish in than
ever. It hides itself less seldom in bushes, but
swirls into deep or rippling pools which invite the
fisherman's fly.

It is a most pleasant wander downstream, with
or without a rod, past Beringen to Mosdorf and
from there to the tiny village near by, Pittange.
The place is the northern outpost of the " anges."
We have seen many a castle set on a hill ; but in
pretty Pittange is one whose builders believed so
in their art as to scorn the reinforcement of strength
which a high-thrown crag gives. The castle was

placed in the valley, and a right stout fortress it was. It had four massive towers, parts of which still exist. The circumference of these must have been 150 feet, and the walls were nearly 10 feet thick. The position of the courtyard can still be fixed. From the centre of it arose a turret, the foundations of which stand a little out of the ground. So high was it that it could be seen from Luxembourg, 15 or 16 kilometres away. A three-arched bridge crossed the foss to the entrance, but that has gone almost. The fosses, too, were much wider and deeper than is usually the case. The castle is part of the Meysembourg estate, and to-day a genial farmer, always ready to show the visitor over the ruins, uses part of the old feudal residence.

Exactly how old the place is, is doubtful, but in early times Pittange's lords were notable people in the land, and they leave a mark in comparatively recent history. One of the family attended as witness the marriage of the Princess Ermesinde, and nearly a century later a member of the house married a great-granddaughter of the Princess. A couple of generations later the domain passed to the famous Lorraine family of Crehange. A descendant married the Count de la Peyrouse, a name which lives in a field of glory widely different from that of his fighting ancestors. One of that name was the explorer of whose expedition, which set out in 1786, some of the sad remains were found half a century later by D'Urville. The castle often bore the full brunt of war. Maximilian of Austria completely destroyed it in 1494, but it was soon rebuilt, and stood until—well, it is not difficult to guess now who wrought the final act of destruction. The little village itself claims to date from early in the tenth century, when it had the somewhat lengthy name of Pittigeromarkum. Where Attert and Alzette join stands Colmar Berg Castle, the country residence of the Grand Ducal family. It is situated in a beautiful park, but it is, unhappily, another instance of tasteless architecture. A castle has stood on the spot since the twelfth century. Prince Henry, who governed the Duchy for William II of the Netherlands, built there a beautiful château in which were preserved the remnants of the ancient building. But its grace and beauty did not please the Grand Duke William, and he rebuilt it. German in everything, this Grand Duke went to the Fatherland for his architects, and the new castle is just about the heaviest and crudest piece of building that could well be imagined. You will be told the style is German, though there is an abundance of descriptive adjectives which do not need capitals and which would be much more appropriate. It is a mixture of everything, with the rococo in evidence over all. Luxembourg stands in very great need of a school of architecture. The visitor's nerves may be soothed, however, by seeing the interior. A visit is permitted if the Grand Ducal family is absent. The furniture is all in beautiful fifteenth-century style, and hints that some one other than the Germanic Grand Duke was responsible for it and its present arrangement.

Three miles away is Ettelbrück.

THE VALLEYS OF EISCH AND MAMER

Sufficient thing—to travel still
Over the plain, beyond the hill.

RUPERT BROOKE.

Let the streams in civil mode
Direct your choice upon a road.

ROBERT LOUIS STEVENSON.

CHAPTER VII

THE VALLEYS OF EISCH AND MAMER

IT is on the Mies Plateau beside Mersch where Alzette, Eisch and Mamer mingle the minstrelsy of their shining pools into one harmonious song. Alzette we already know—Lorraine-born, proud of its lengthy course and, rightly, of its never-fading beauty from its youth at Esch to old age at Ettelbrück. So now there remain to our wandering footsteps the valleys of Eisch and Mamer. Both are Luxembourg streams entirely, rising within a couple of kilometres of each other, trickling from opposite sides of the same mountain, flowing apart until thirteen kilometres of field and forest separate them, running for miles on either side of a tree-covered barrier, and finding an end at last in the "Sure's provider." On the Mies Plateau, therefore, we shall fall in with the advice of R. L. S. and let them "direct our choice upon a road." Seldom will the taking of that advice lead you wrong in our Ruritania.

The plateau is a delightful spot, with a wide extent of waving grass and trees, especially beautiful when it is "crisp with the silver autumn morns distil" and the air is laden with the flowers' perfume. We shall ascend the castled Eisch and descend the Mamer.

It must certainly always be a matter for wonder that such a small country as Luxembourg could contain, in the olden days, such a goodly number of seigneurs, give them armies, and provide them with that wealth necessary to maintain their castles and enable them to indulge their generally high ideas of how noble lords of the time should live and enjoy themselves. Not even Rhineland can, in proportion, show so many old castles. The first we encounter on this route is that of Hollenfels, rising on a huge rock crowned with a thick cluster of trees. Now, I have often virtually requested you to call down maledictions upon the name of the redoubtable Marshal Boufflers ; here I must, in common justice, ask you to render him thanks, though not too jubilantly, and to associate with that praise the name—I honestly admit I do not know it—of the lord of the Hollow Rock at that particular period. For between them they saved the magnificent castle, so that to-day it remains the most perfectly preserved of the Duchy fortresses of old. Boufflers certainly marched against it " with malice aforethought " and put his artillery in position. The lord of the castle watched the operation with ever-increasing anxiety. Boufflers gave the word, and whizzing through the morning air came the first warlike call to surrender. The gun was extremely well laid, and the shot made an ugly dent in the wall. How very good the aim was you can see to-day, for the mark remains. So

IN THE VALLEY OF THE EISCH.

To face p. 245.

terrified was my lord that the castle of his pride should come clattering down about his ears that he hastily had the gate opened and the drawbridge lowered. Then he hastened to the bold bombarder with, " I bring thee here my fortress keys." It was not, for Boufflers, a very glorious victory, though it was an easy one. As reward for saving trouble the lord of the castle was allowed to keep his proud abode intact.

To-day no lordly or craven warrior has it, but an amiable and stalwart farmer, and he is only too pleased to see visitors and to entertain them. Climb up the steep forest road that leads to it and let him act as your guide. The castle is beautifully preserved. The delightful façade is, I should say, sixteenth century, but probably when the hurried surrender took place (1683) much of the fortress was of recent construction. It has a huge square tower, loopholed and strong ; the Salle des Chevaliers is large—evidently the sires of Hollenfels were liberal entertainers. A wall runs along to another tower, round, which is also well preserved, and so are the chapel, the underground passages and the various household apartments, all the latter being quite spacious. Ditches run round the building, the size and strength of which tells of an important family. And so, indeed, these seigneurs were, and time and again their names are written big in Luxembourg's history. In unbroken succession from at least 1192 —that is the earliest date of which there is a definite historical record—until about 1800 these sires held sway over a domain, and their power, if it experienced varying fortunes, was never to be altogether despised even at the ebb of fickle fortune.

Down again from this ancient phantom sharply grey, lying in a most beautiful, slumberous mantle of restful green and gold, and we reach the road once more. Forward lies the route, round to the right, and as you turn the corner greet the hard-working young women who, at the old public open-air "laundry," which served their great-grand-mothers, are busy with the family washing. And now we are within sight of the Abbey of Marienthal which I have mentioned several times already. There are many vales of peace in our little Grand Duchy, but here is the queen of them all—Mary's Vale. And what name could be more suggestive of rest and of quiet? It is curious that the noise of the outside world has never entered here ; that all the storms of seven militant centuries have beat around and in it in vain and left its calm undisturbed, though Nature gave it no protecting barrier like that of Esch. Quiet is the stream which runs by it and seems to bate its breath in so doing ; warlike seigneurs, anti-Roman Catholic fury, scores of armies searching for battle and the devastating sweep of vandalism which the French Revolution sent over the Grand Duchy—all these have worked their havoc in and around this peaceful vale. Yet still it reposes a nest of dreams.

Here there once stood a convent for the daughters of noble families. The present remains of the early abbey which took the place of the convent are but few, for the original abbey building probably dates from the year 1237 or thereabouts. It was one of the lords of Mersch who founded it, and Ermesinde, whom you will not have forgotten, did not omit it from the long list of the religious houses which that noble lady endowed of her charity and her wealth. Then the Countess Yolande of Vianden, Sainte Yolande—daughter of Henry I and of Marguerite of Courteney, of the House of Namur which gave emperors to Imperial Byzantium—fleeing from home and a hateful marriage, found refuge here, became abbess, dying in 1283, leaving a sainted name for piety and good works among the people, and living long enough to be able to offer to her mother a refuge in her old age. Both ladies were buried in the abbey, and long after their tombs, with graven figures upon them, were found again.

The abbey of to-day is, of course, a modern building. The old convent, after being suppressed by Joseph II, that Don Juan-like ruler, suffered severely at the hands of the French vandals, much of the material being taken to build the Grand Ducal summer residence which still stands at Walferdange on the Alzette between Luxembourg and Mersch. At the turn of the road you look down upon the abbey garden, and see a fragment of the wall that still stands. And round across the river at the entrance there still stands some of the ancient building. Enter? Why, of course !

I can never forget the first time I made the acquaintance of the venerable Father who rules the abbey in the Vale of Peace. I had come by a way across the fields and through the woods from the

valley of the Mamer, and as I approached the vale
I met the Father with a number of the novices.
What a striking figure he made ! He was clad in a
white robe and wore a red fez and a string of dark
beads round his shoulders. He looked like a figure
which had stepped out of a picture in an old Bible.
The swarthy hue given by a North African sun made
him look almost more Biblical ; he was tall, with
finely chiselled features—a commanding figure he
would have been in any surroundings and in any
garb. To my salute he raised a blessing hand and
then stopped to talk. We returned to the abbey, and
I was shown over it. Then we walked in the garden,
the centre from which radiates the wondrous peace
of the vale. The Father is of the Order of the White
Fathers of Africa, who, from Algiers, have long
waged the battles of the Cross in the northern part
of the Dark Continent. And the young men who
are being trained here in the abbey are destined to
reinforce that army of peace. How well they are
trained for their future work ! And what a magnificent place the abbey is to train them in ! What
memories it will leave in their hearts, this Vale of
Peace, when African sands and an African sun can
give them nothing so restful and so beautiful as the
old garden where the gentle Eisch flows ! The
venerable Father has had his share of warfare for
his faith. Right into the very heart of Africa he
has carried the Word as he believes it. One of the
rooms of the abbey looks like that of an African
explorer, with its shields and weapons from the far
shores of Victoria Nyanza and the dark parts of

remotest Africa. I found it hard to leave this garden, wine-warm and lovely with many-coloured flowers. To me it must always remain a " garden that I love," a memory of quiet delight, clear and fadeless. Once more a blessing hand and a hearty " good-bye," which, we too often forget, is a blessing, and I set off again on my way up the river.

Past another turn or two of the road, and towering high above all around is the castle of Ansembourg. At the foot of it a little village clusters, and as I had gone the greater part of the day without anything to eat I ventured into a tiny inn. Oh, but the fare was rough ! At ordinary times I might have turned up my nose at it, but now I had plenty of the sauce which hunger provides. And, indeed, a Luxembourg appetite pardons much. In quiet Luxembourg you go into the inn, too, just for that reason for which in London and other bustling places you buy a newspaper—to get the news. And I got it in this case, and a guide as well.

The Ansembourg family no longer lives in the donjon high ; like one or two more of the descendants of ancient races, their desire for the up to date has overcome their veneration for the old and historic. So, just before you come within sight of the castle height, there is the new residence to be seen, a fine modern building with a beautiful French garden running down to the river. If it had not been for my guide I think I should have taken old Ansembourg for granted, and at once pushed farther on, so high up and difficult of attainment it appears to be when viewed from the road. But Monsieur

Guide was a jolly fellow and " of infinite jest." His stories made the stiff climb seem an easy one, and soon we reached the historic ruin on its imposing rock in which time has cut many a deep crevasse.

Old Boufflers was not so kind to this fortress as he was to that of the Hollow Rock, nor, indeed, was the Count of Ansembourg the faint-hearted defender that the lord of Hollenfels was when he heard the French cannon summon him to surrender. He set up the best defence he could, but had to give in. He did not do so, however, before Boufflers with his heavy artillery had made the place untenable. The castle-destroyer-in-chief, then, is responsible for the tragic state in which this ancient building finds itself. How old the castle is does not appear to be exactly certain, but it is perhaps one of the most recent and yet one of the first to be abandoned by its owners. In the fifteenth century there were seigneurs of Ansembourg, but not till the eighteenth century did they receive the dignity of count. The ancient lords were not of the ambitious metal of most of their neighbours ; they stirred up few quarrels and took part in as little warfare as possible. In present-day times Counts of Ansembourg are in the diplomatic service of the State.

It is an awe-inspiring ruin, Ansembourg on the height. The years have thrown an ivy mantle over it, as though thinking that in its old age it should be decently garbed. Trees ward off the winds and, alas ! largely shut out the view up and down the river. And still some of its highest walls remain. Some say it was abandoned after it had received

Photo by] [F. Scharff Vandiver, Luxembourg.

ANSEMBOURG CASTLE.

To face p. 254.

Boufflers' unwelcome attentions, and, if that be so, it is really wonderful that walls which must be considerably over two hundred feet high should be standing and still boldly defying winds and winter storms. Ramparts still frown almost every whit as angry-looking as when they were the target for French cannon. The façade still preserves much of its nobility. Halls are rubbish-strewn, the chapel might well be restored to something like decent order. The rugged fortress is a weirdly picturesque pile truly worth preserving, for it stands in most appropriately grim surroundings. At times it looks like a castle lifted out of an Aubrey Beardsley picture, a vast page torn from an immense fairy-book. Then again, when dark clouds lower upon it, this deep-enskied keep appears to be one down from which Wiertz might send his dragons and giants sprawling.

Not exactly a place to live in, you may think ! But some one does not agree. A farmer has his abode in this ghoulish height, and he told me that for nearly a couple of centuries his people had lived and worked there. Then my guide led me down again by a little-frequented path and said that I must see the smithy. I replied that I had already seen it en passant, but that was not enough for him. I must see it to appreciate the story that is told about it, a story of which the good democratic people of the neighbourhood are extremely proud. It reminded me of a faintly remembered story of very long ago, of the proud lord who was annoyed by the clang of the anvil not far from his castle and who employed some very underhand trick to get rid of the

annoyance. What exactly the plan was I have forgotten, but it was one not very well calculated to
give one a high opinion of old nobility.

Well, probably the story came from this part of
the world, for up on his rocky height an old seigneur
of 'Ansembourg was kept awake at nights by the
hammer, hammer, hammer of the diligent smith.
The smith—be it interpolated—must have been a
Thor in his craft to send a sleep-breaking clang up
yonder height, but—well, we are dealing with a story
and with romantic times. Let it be assumed then that
the count was disturbed. His lordship informed
the smith, Rollingen by name, that the annoyance
must be ended or he would drag the disturber of
the peace before the administrator of the law. But,
as my guide would have it, Rollingen was a demo-
crat. He feared not the seigneur, and he had some
knowledge of the law. He was, too, of a romantic
mind and not unambitious, for all his lowly stock.
So he answered the lord of the castle in this wise.
He would not stop his noise, and his hammer would
yet accomplish more marvellous things than the
making of horseshoes. His hammer, indeed, was to
be mightier than the sword, and it would conquer,
before much time had passed, the very castle itself.
The story does not relate to us what the noble lord
of the grim rock said on receiving this reply. Evidently he did nothing, however, for the smith continued to hammer away upon his anvil. Then the
seigneur lived his alloted span and was gathered
into the resting-place of his fathers. I give it as
the guide's solution of this part of the story that the

law, being famous nowhere for the absence of delay, was in those days an even slower affair, and that the seigneur did not live long enough to allow of the matter being brought into court.

Be all that as it may ; time passed, the smith flourished, and the count died. With the seigneur's death the male line of that particular branch of the family came to an end. The only survivor of it was a daughter, and she inherited all the broad acres and the proud castle of Ansembourg. Now you know the rest of the story. There was a lady in the case when the bold smith penned his letter to the angry seigneur. She—the count's daughter, in very truth—persuaded the smith not to mention that fact to any one, least of all to the seigneur himself. And, besides, "they were in no hurry." But when the lady became her own mistress and lady of Ansembourg, why, there was no reason why there should not be marriage bells. And marriage bells there were from the chapel of the castle itself. And, indeed, the Ansembourg line has to thank the hammer more than the sword for the fact that the nobility of the Grand Duchy still includes amongst it a Count of Ansembourg.

The road, with beautiful woods on either hand, sweeps in a south-westerly direction and across the Eisch. Then suddenly it almost doubles on its path, across the river you go again, and in a few minutes the quaint little village of Bour is reached. There is nothing, unless he has a rugged appetite, to keep the wanderer any time in the village. It is now five or six kilometres to the next of Eisch's castles, that of Septfontaines, or, which is the same thing come by a different way, Simmern. Simmern is a local boiling down of Siebenborn, *i.e.*, Seven Springs. I believe that there are seven springs hereabouts which flow into the Eisch, but I have not worried to count them, as one can always take the word of the people of old in such matters.

It is impossible to tell whether Boufflers bombarded this castle or not, and it had been several years in ruins when the French troops came along during the Revolution. The stories of how it became a ruin vary a good deal, some saying that it was blown up as the result of a sort of local gunpowder plot. More likely, however, is the statement that a herd-boy, either by accident or design, set fire to it. At any rate, there it stands to-day, a great, scorched, solemn-looking ruin, upon a height reached by steep paths. The climber is rewarded by a magnificent view of the surrounding country-side. The castle is a particularly old one, and its early history is "wropt in mystery." You can find traces which tell you that, as on the plateau of Dalheim, "Rome was here." A formidable place it was in the day of its might, as you can see from the charred and blackened ruins of to-day, a colossal feudal stronghold round which many a stubborn fight must have raged. It was undoubtedly the greatest of the western fortresses of the Grand Duchy, and was within the territory, for a long time, of the Counts of Arlon, who were the great people of this particular region.

The little church is the work of a friend of Henry VII, Grand Duke of Luxembourg and

Emperor of Germany, and the old man who showed me over it avowed that the builder had so far forgotten himself as to give to the Christ the features of the ruler whom he had served for some time before taking holy orders, and that the group in the choir also represents persons living at the time, the fourteenth century, who were the friends of the builder, one Thomas de Septfontaines. The old man, too, had a long Borgian story to tell me of the death of this particular Henry, and he wished to know if I had ever come across any confirmation of it in all the history I had read. I had to confess that I had not, and to add that the unravelling of ancient poison mysteries was not a pastime of which I was fond. Whereat the old gentleman produced a tattered guide-book from which he read me a long story of the poisoning of Henry at Mass by a priest who, it was more than merely likely, had been urged to his dark deed by the very person who had built Septfontaines' little Gothic chapel. A king of France and some obscurely royal personage of some other country were said to be behind the business, so I have little doubt that the story which interested the old man had a good deal of truth in it.

Septfontaines is the last of the Eisch Valley castles, but the fact that all the ancient glories set up by men are at an end does not by any means imply that we are at the end of the attractiveness of this part of the little Duchy. On the contrary. If the visitor is in the mood for a delightful tramp, he cannot do better than shoulder a Rücksack and trace the Eisch to its source. It is not " a straight path,

my wanderers," but for those who like a glorious
tramp through delightful country here is a little
nook in our lovely Ruritania that will provide it.
So hurry on to Hobscheid and seek repose at the inn
there. Be up and ready for the way by sunrise,
when the air is crisp and walking feels to be the
one thing in all the world, and when the amethystine
wave of the dawn is throwing its tide upon the
mountain-tops.

Attractive roads are of two kinds in the real
wanderer's view. First there is that that rises and
falls, bringing now a struggle to reach the height,
then, like a siesta in the warmth of day, the slope,
an easy and restful saunter down again to valleys
and rivers and greener trees. The true tramp is
not like some modern town builders ; he does not
want long vistas. He likes a road that will lure
him on now with height and now with vale, not
being prodigal of too many of its charms at one time,
but presenting them one by one and always keeping
something hidden behind the next turning, something that calls. For so a road is like life. There is
always something unknown and untasted, and, as that
makes life what it is, so the eternal secret of the
road gives it that attractive nature which the way
in front must always have to the eyes and to the
imagination of him who truly loves a road.

But it is not this kind of road that I offer the
wanderer now. That which shares the sauntering
and the song of the Eisch is no height-climbing way,
but what it loses by being fairly level it wins back
again by twists and errant rambles through forests,

so that little by little the traveller by it knows what delights it has in store for him. It is still the Eisch-climbing main road by which you travel westwards from Hobscheid, and with the Grossbusch woods on the right and the river and the fields on the other side, it goes gently twisting until Eischen is reached, a little beyond the railway line. Any one will tell you the woodland way from there to Steinfort. River and railway are crossed again, and beside the station you leave them to run along the frontier for a little while and take the more easterly path which goes at times under the shade of trees and at others on the outskirt of the woods with the verdant heights spreading themselves all around. For a summer forenoon there are few more pleasant tramps in the Grand Duchy than this border wander between Eisch and Steinfort, amid fairest greenery with the jewel-flash of the sun upon the landscape.

At Steinfort the path joins the main road between Arlon and Luxembourg, one of those very excellent roads for which this part of the Continent is famous, and which make it an ideal locality for the cyclist to tour. There are several inns which will provide satisfaction for the appetite which the walk from Eischen has created, and a ramble round the pretty little town will prepare the tourist for the next étape of the way. Steinfort lies crowded quite picturesquely on both banks of the river, its quaint-looking houses fitting almost exactly into an accommodating bend. There is a direct way south to the small town of Kleinbettingen, which is an important railway centre, the middle of a spider's web of lines, but the way

I took one sunny afternoon is, I think, much to be preferred.

I simply followed where the river led, sometimes having odd scrambles for my trouble, and reaching a tiny place called, if I remember rightly, Kahler, which is little more than a railway station. It had a good road to tempt me, but I adhered to my companion the river until I reached Grass. Here there was a somewhat different choice of routes. I could either keep on following the river, which had the railway for company, or take the main road, which struck straight through a forest. But it was getting late, so I inquired for an inn. There was none. Que faire? Take the train to Kleinbettingen, one person was good enough to suggest, but that was like beating a retreat. Well, then, take it in the other way to Clémency, said another of the mildly interested peasants to whom I was talking. I looked at the map. The name Clémency had an attractive sound, but when I put my finger on it on the map a third person in the crowd ventured to suggest that there was no such place. Oh yes, there was, another added, and it was only four or five kilometres away. Still the other would have it that there was something wrong, and that he had never heard of the place.

There it was on the map, however, and off I set in the gathering twilight to find it. The way dived straight into darkening woods, all silent save for the occasional scamper of some late-prowling little animal. It was delightfully cool, and going was easy and invigorating. Along came an old farmer's labourer, joining the road from a side-path. Out of curiosity I asked him if he knew where such a place as Clémency happened to be. He expressed ignorance, and, looking upon me as a suspicious character, he went on with a growled "good-night." The matter was getting very strange, and no mistake. Here the map showed a town a few kilometres away ; here was a finger-post supplying information as to the places in the opposite direction ; and passers-by were looking on me with suspicion.

Another inhabitant appeared before the previous one had got out of sight, and I asked him a different question.

" What is the name of the next town? " I inquired, after an evening salutation.

" Oh, Kuentzig, you mean? " was the reply.

" Yes, I suppose I do, if it is also called Clémency."

" Well, some people call it that, but the German railway people call it Kuentzig, and that name appears to be more generally used than the other."

And the moral to those that wander is that it is advisable to remember that many towns in our Duchy have two names. But it was certainly curious to come across a German name right on the French border where the German character of the people, once evident enough no doubt, had entirely disappeared. Yet Kleinbettingen, not many miles away, might have warned me.

So at Clémency I found a passable abode for the night, and was up with the dawn again.

There are not many more delightful views than that which you will see if you are up early enough to watch the sun rise over the eastern hill that guards Clémency. It is Mount Mauerchen, the Mountain of the Little Wall. Taking the Mamer road, you cross the stream near the station. Go on till you find a pathway cutting off at right angles—that on the left leads to a little village with the name of Fingig—and in less than a quarter of an hour you should find the spot where the long-traced Eisch has its rise. Westward you look to where Clémency lies on the outskirts of a mass of green forestland ; you can see the twisting river and the railway that twists with it, for the engineers who made the iron way knew that, as the river took the line of least resistance, they would save themselves much boring and cutting if they too took it for guide. It is not often that engineers are so wise ; generally they delight in running their heads against a wall till they get through. So if our Grand Duchy has a railway that would annoy the hustler with its twists and turns, it has one here which brings pleasure to the wanderer who must travel by it, since it runs beside and not through Nature's beauties.

The source of a stream ! Is it not, my wanderers, an event? But to-day we shall mark with two such white stones. We shall find the rising point of the Mamer as well. That of the Eisch is, perhaps, the most interesting, for it is curious to think what a twisting course, what historic ground the water trickling from the little mountain-side must know before it reaches the plateau of Mies and, introducing itself to Mamer and Alzette, accompanies them to the Sure. Septfontaines, Ansembourg, Marienthal, Hollenfels—

these are the proud places which it has in its course, and there is no need why the Eisch should envy any other river.

Mamer is a stream of a different sort. From the same "Little Wall Mountain" it comes, but it flows to its destination with determined directness. Let us seek the spot which sees its rise. Climb over the "Little Wall" and you reach a path through the fields back to the main Mamer road. Down the slope and in a quarter of an hour you are in the little village of Hivange. There any one will tell you where the source is, and it is quite near. Along the valley the river and the Mamer road run together, the latter delightfully shaded with trees and the former learning how to sing. Only too soon you will hear the noise of the railway again and behold a station which informs you that the town lying over there has taken its name from the river. There is no reason for remaining in Mamer—a fairly busy little place which is scattered on both sides of the highway—and besides there is a wood ahead offering a much more pleasant midday halting-place than any inn. This wood goes by various names. If you take the path along the river-side you are soon marching along with the forest on your right. That is the Strassenbusch. And when the trees close in on the left, too, the addition is the Juckelbusch. On the right, beyond the Strassenbusch, is the huge forest of Baumbusch, stretching away till it touches the outskirts of the city of Luxembourg.

Right from here to the plateau of Mies road and river run together through this green paradise. After

Kopstal, where the wanderer may stay the night, the forests break up into sections, and many paths lead alluringly into the greenwood. The river, too, is an excellent one for the angler. In fact, from Mamer downstream to Mersch the wanderer cannot do better than go rod in hand. The river is all free, and he can be certain of a good " kill." The trout in the river, at least so is my experience, are not very large, but both quantity and quality will more than recompense the fisherman for the small individual size of the fish which will be fatally attracted by his bait. Fishing, too, takes one slowly through this delightful piece of country, and it is well to go leisurely in this corner of the Duchy, for it is rich in spots of particular charm to the naturelover, and to hustle through it is really wantonness.

If time does not permit the visitor to make such an extended tour in this part of the country, then a good plan is to retrace one's steps either at Ansembourg or Septfontaines back again to Marienthal and take the bypath which leads across country, via the delightfully situated farm of Klaushof, and reach the Mamer-Mersch road at Schönfels. Schönfels— the last of the castles of this region—is called by the natives Schindels, which again is doubtless derived from the ancient name of the fortress, which was Schindalesheim and later Schonvels. There is a difference of opinion as to which height here is entitled to the name. The castle is certainly called by that name, but there is another rocky eminence a little distance away to the left which some say is the real Beautiful Rock. This rock is said to have got its name from one of the ladies of the manor of old on account of the fact that her son one day fell over it but was guarded in his fall by a guardian angel, so that he was found by his wellnigh despairing mother sitting at the foot of the crag as though nothing had happened.

That happening is said to be the reason for the existence of the little chapel which stands on the rock facing the castle on the other. In the same rock is a grotto which is called the " Grotte des Nains," and also the " Vichtelsloch." This particular race of dwarfs went by the name of Nutons, and the story has it that they overran the whole country at one time. Their reputation, unlike that of most of such little folks, was a good one, and many tales are told of the good those small people did by stealth when the world was young, when benefactors had little difficulty in shunning advertisement and seldom had to blush to find their good deeds made the basis of fame. And there is their home. I must leave the wanderer to explore it for himself and see if the grotto is the entrance to an underworld Ruritania, as the good people in the neighbourhood will have it that it is.

And now up to the castle. A huge place it must have been, and an awe-inspiring one in the long-lost days of its pristine might. There, too, is the serf village crouching closely to the protecting fortress. In reading the history of Luxembourg the name of the seigneurs of Schönfels is nearly always encountered when " there is throats to be cut and work to be done." A particularly large number of neighbouring lords, too, appears to have had scores to wipe out with the bold barons of the Rock Beautiful. Often was the place attacked, and several times taken, and its owners, down to the sixteenth century, when the domain passed out of the hands of the original family, the lords of Schönfels, were seldom without warlike work to do, either as the attacking party or as the attacked.

Still the castle stands on its high-flung, wind-braving rock, kept, happily, in fairly good repair by the Goethals family, into whose hands it has come. Swarthy with age are its many parapets, but strong are the walls of the great and imposing donjon, to the top of which the visitor can climb, be he so minded, by a rough staircase of a hundred and seven steps. His energy will certainly be rewarded, for not only is there a fine bird's-eye view of the castle to be obtained, but a magnificently beautiful stretch of country lies all around. At no time is the surrounding country-side, river and valley and height, more charming than when the impetuous purples from the sky of peace make the evening gorgeous and the wind's inexplicable tune plays lightly among the trees and the ruins. True, those who have restored the fortress have not been quite so tasteful as they might have been, but that they have restored it at all must be counted to them for credit. The porch of the donjon is a crude and unnecessary sort of thing, and the venerable ruin was in no need of the modern windows which have been put into it. Still, it is as fine a relic of that greatness of Luxembourg whose might is spent, and as you leave it and tramp down the valley towards Mersch many a time will you turn to look back again at the towering fortress of the Beautiful Rock.

The forest on the left dies away ; yonder rise the tower and the church spires of Mersch again, and you follow the river into the quiet little town, bringing with you an appetite for the Brandenbourg Hotel's jugged hare, which will require not a little satisfying. And if you are wise and have an eye to the future you will bring with you Mamer trout to vary the feast. But at any rate you will cherish in your memory innumerable pictures of two of the loveliest streams which flow through our beautiful little Ruritania.

VIANDEN AND ITS NEIGHBOUR-HOOD

Here sprawls the earth, in chaos hurled—
Brute fastness of a ruder world—
Couched dragonlike with spine and horn,
And flushed with fury eve and morn.

A. C. Benson.

CHAPTER VIII

VIANDEN AND ITS NEIGHBOURHOOD

WHERE the Alzette finds, with the Wark, extinction in the all-consuming Sure, stands Ettelbrück. The name, as I have explained, means Attila's Bridge. Though doubtless "the Goths' wide-wandering camp" was pitched everywhere in this neighbourhood, there is no proof that the great "finder of the sword of Mars," who claimed to be ruler of the Barbarians from the North Sea to the dim confines of the Celestial Empire, ever built a bridge here or even passed through the place. But a town can scarcely be asked to change its name for any such paltry reason. His followers, of course, might have so named the place as an honour to their ruler. But why is not apparent ; there is not and never was anything distinct or distinguished about the place. It was never a fort ; it never had a castle. However, that is their affair.

A long, rambling town, it is industrial and an important railway junction ; it has an agricultural college famed beyond the borders of the Grand Duchy, a retreat for the aged, a monthly cattle fair and a church. Everything about it suggests the

15

town with no history. The church looks old and worn from the outside but is surprisingly beautiful inside, and in its calm you forget its annoying architecture, in which the builder has endeavoured to be Roman and modern at the same time—an attempt made rather too often in Luxembourg.

On account of all that, however, do not leave Ettelbrück severely alone. It is a capital centre for excursions in the north-eastern corner of the Duchy. Its hotels are good ; three railways and three rivers and thrice as many roads make the ugly little town their centre, and railway, river and road can satisfy all tastes in travel. To the north spreads the Osling ; southward is the region of the Alzette and its tributaries. The Vianden and Echternach regions lie eastwards, and to the west the lovely land between the rivers Wiltz and Attert. Ettelbrück, indeed, is a better wander-centre than Vianden.

But just a moment before we leave. One morning the landlady greeted me with : " Il y aura beaucoup de monde partout aujourd'hui." And why? Because it was " le grand jour de fête "—Grosse Kermesse. A delightful September sun was shining, and trains brought hundreds and hundreds of people from all parts of the district. Religious observances over on a feast day, Ettelbrück, twice its size for the time, settles down, with talk and laughter, to enjoy the two things for which the place has no little fame. Dinner begins with jugged hare and ends with plum-tart. The hare, supposed to be responsible for Easter eggs, should really be an Easter dish, but Ettelbrück, like other places, has got so fond of it that large quantities of this somewhat heavy fare are consumed on all high days and holidays and even private "glad and jolly days." The Luxembourg plum-tart is a much more distinctive production ; it varies in size, but your Luxembourger likes it large. On the pastry, light as Vienna bread, plums cut lengthwise are placed in circles till the whole is covered ; sugar is plentifully scattered over them, and the tart is put in the oven for a short while. During the plum season there is no getting away from this somewhat primitive dainty ; at breakfast, lunch and dinner it occupies no small portion of the table. It is tasty and refreshing—if you avoid jugged hare !

There is a good main road, as well as a railway, to Diekirch ; but there is also a woodland pathway of which no guide-book tells, and which, as far as I know, no map deigns to show. On the opposite side of the river from the town rises a little mountain called the Nouck, the western extremity of a wooded highland which runs on the south side of the Sure from Ettelbrück to Diekirch. At either end there is a " pavillon," that on the Nouck being finely placed and offering a beautiful view along this woodland to Diekirch. A path runs, zigzag, from one height to the other, another of those glorious ramble-ways in which the Grand Duchy is so rich. It passes above the village of Ingeldorf, lying on the left bank of the Sure, where are still to be found some remains of a bridge built by the Romans. After leaving the outskirts of the village the path mounts again, plunges right across the height of land, and then, after a right-angle turn, goes straight forward towards the eastern eminence, the Hart, one of the most charming view-points in this part of the country. Especially is the landscape surrounding the town beautiful when the soft flame of morning and evening is upon wood and hill and river, when Nature, lovely colourist, shows us all the rapture that is autumn— a memory-haunting vision.

If you go exploring round Diekirch there is no getting away from things Celtic. The Hart has many a " mardelle," a slight hollow, the almost obliterated excavation in which the rude Celt had his home. And just on the fringe of the wood, towards Diekirch—the word itself is from Didekirch, *i.e.*, the Church of Dido, or Dide [1]—stands a huge menhir. It consists of two piles close together, each of five large, roughly hewn stones. There are two great blocks on the top, the uppermost being pointed. This relic of Celtic times is known by two different names ; one is Deivelselter, or Devil's Altar, and the other Didoselter (or Dideselter), the Altar of Dido. Personally I prefer the latter, but people who can find among the dents and roughness of the great stones something that looks like a cloven foot hold that it was erected to his Satanic majesty. I think something more of the Celts than that, and I believe they were more likely to raise their rough tribute to the goddess of Beauty, of Love and of Marriage. The original megalith fell to ruins in 1815 before the onslaught of the weather. In ruins

---

[1] This is not Virgil's Dido, but the granddaughter of Odin and the niece of Thor.

it lay for over thirty years, and then the reconstruction was a matter of difficulty owing to the fact that only a dim idea existed of what the "altar" was originally like. Of the twelve stones of which it is composed five are new, including the roughly pointed top. During the excavations at the time of the restoration part of a skeleton was found, together with a few examples of the crudest and oldest pottery. Some authorities say that the skeleton is that of the first victim to be slaughtered here in sacrifice to the gods.

From the menhir a delightful view of Diekirch and the surrounding country-side is to be had, the sight penetrating on a clear day as far as to Bourscheid Castle, nine kilometres across country, a grey mass against the blue of distance. And not only in the rough altar have the rearers of it left traces of themselves. The names they gave to villages, brooks and heights have survived. Christianity has turned Thorenberg to Herrenberg, but the God of War is still honoured in such names as Bellenflesschen, Bollendorf, Behlendorf and Behlenberg.

Diekirch lies on the left of the wide valley of the Sure, protected by an amphitheatre of encircling heights. Tradition is liberal in the age it bestows upon the place. Too liberal, people said, until one day down by the river near the bridge was found a medallion which proved to be one of that Roman Emperor who is known in history by his nickname— Caracalla, son of Septimus Severus, the Emperor who died at York in 211. With that medallion it would really be a poor and unimaginative town which could not construct a story of imperial favour and staggering antiquity. And Diekirch certainly played its part well in history. It fought bravely against all foes. Its walls were reared by John of Bohemia, and, centuries later, Boufflers the Eternal was surprised to see the besieged coolly repairing, under a hot fire, the damage which his guns had caused! A century ago the walls were razed, and where they ran there are now shady boulevards.

The most curious thing about Diekirch is that the old town stands out perfectly distinct and still guards its ancient characteristics. The border-line between old and new is quite clear. The ancient streets with huddled houses, the narrow culs-de-sac, are crowded together in the centre of the town, while round about the new spreads in open order and with ample space. Hidden in one of the culs-de-sac, in the centre of the town, stands the ancient church of St. Laurent—a venerable building in a pitiful state of decay. It has the marks of four different centuries upon it. The nave on the northern side at the left dates from the ninth century, the time of Charlemagne. That part was probably all the primitive building of that time consisted of. The great portion of the building as it stands to-day is sixteenth-century work, though the façade is probably two hundred years younger. In 1758 a fire destroyed the spire, which was rebuilt shortly afterwards. It is a great pity that such an old church—the oldest in this part of the country—should crumble to ruins. When I was last in it some poor efforts at restoration were evidently being made ;

dust from the roof was falling thickly over all ;
a little box was there for those who liked to help
the work forward, but it was empty. For eleven
hundred years here has been holy ground. Even
to-day, amid the dust, the decay and the darkness,
there is a majesty of peace, a fascination in the
edifice which not all the harmonies of architecture
and colour and light and order can always ensure.

At the entrance to the cul-de-sac, and almost hiding
it, stands the Hotel de Ville—just about the crudest
piece of architecture I have ever seen. It is really
frightful. But it was presented to the town by the
proprietor—the person, no doubt, mainly responsible
for the crazy piece of work ; and the people of
Diekirch, good souls, fall back on the saying : " A
cheval donné on ne regarde pas à la bride." So,
without enthusiasm, they term it " le château de
Diekirch." I shall leave the new church of St.
Laurent alone, for to talk of it would only be to
become angry in adjectives about more bad architecture.

A kernel of antiquity in a modern shell, Diekirch
has little in itself that is of interest to show ; it is
its surroundings that charm and attract. Its people
are most enthusiastic anglers—so much so that they
fish with five or six rods at a time ! But angling
information has its place elsewhere.[1] At no part of
its long course does the Sure pass through such
delightful country as at this part. Go down the wide
valley to Gilsdorf and you cannot but admire the
fine green of the rolling fields and the picturesque

[1] See Chapter X.

hills, a delightful contrast to the ruggedness and chaos which is to be seen higher upstream and farther down as well. Beyond the village is a choice of rambles. On the right side the dainty little Sasselbach runs with a song into the Sure, after having bickered down a charmingly rugged little valley, and the path up the gorge leads to the Fels-Medernach-Diekirch route.

Farther down on the other side of the river the Blees contributes to the waters of the Sure, and a road runs with the stream, crossing and recrossing it, till Brandenbourg is reached. High above (450 metres) towers the Herrenberg. A path leads up to the top from the Blees Valley, and it is said that on a clear day you can count thirty villages lying around Diekirch. I cannot vouch for the accuracy of the figure, for, to my mind, arithmetic and scenery go very badly together. But the sight of that landscape from the top of the Herrenberg, or even from the platform kindly placed some distance up, that parterre of prettiest colours, is something to enjoy and remember. Down again, and an apple-tree-bordered road leads onward. This is a little-known route, but, to my mind, it leads through one of the most attractive parts of the Duchy. A road with apple-trees on either side and a river singing near—that is a wanderer's joy, surely. And that talkative river has a name it deserves, an endearing diminutive, for Blees has been run together out of By-laes, which means " little river." It ripples down from a plateau fifteen kilometres north from the Sure, and, like a true wanderer, it twists that fifteen out to twenty.

And it enjoys life all the way. It frisks over innumerable cascades ; it acted as a guard for one side of Brandenbourg Castle when the foe came, and provided water for the deep fosse on the other. And were I an enthusiastic angler, it is in the Little River that I should fish, for it is the most sporting river of all the Grand Duchy.

You pass little Bastendorf—a score of tiny houses round a spired fourteenth-century church, with flowers, fertile fields and little gardens. And, in addition, it is just here that you cross a frontier which no map shows ; you go from Gutland to Osling. You leave smiles for frowns, and the Little River, which sings past both, makes music in more dulcet tones below Bastendorf. It was the sea that made Gutland, and through Bastendorf the shoreline passed. Blees, having danced along on a path of schist, takes a way of sandstone ; it leaves the last of the tall poplars and begins to water apple-trees ; it comes from shadow to sunshine, from one sounding-board to another of a different kind, which softens and sweetens its rollicking lay. You cannot help seeing the difference ; you can feel it if you taste air as a wine-taster tastes wine. The valley becomes narrower, the heights lose their soft and radiant charm, the whole aspect of the country becomes severe with real northern dignity. The sea calmed the passion of the southern lands, but in the north streams and rain and wind and snow wrought them into the chaos they are to-day.

Then you come upon Brandenbourg, on its rugged height by the river. Luxembourg knew few more powerful fortresses, because she had few more rugged heights in her length and breadth. It was well to know which side the lord of Brandenbourg chose before any ducal overlord settled upon a policy or called for an army. It was reared in the twelfth century, and, until Boufflers appeared suddenly one morning before it, rulers of Luxembourg " kept their eye on Brandenbourg " with very much greater anxiety than English politicians were supposed to have concerning the moods and doings of Paisley. It was the Lancashire of Luxembourgian history. And many a fierce siege and assault were directed against it, and though it had to give in on some occasions it was always defended valiantly.

And when you look at it to-day, surely, you think, Boufflers was something of an artist. He came upon a grim Brandenbourg, and he left it in picturesque ruins ; he blackened it here and knocked away a sharp angle there. And he gave the bushes and firs time and room to grow within and without, and from them now the towers, with the connecting walls, rise in a way which makes the castle dear to him who loves a picture. In the wall on the right of the castle entrance is still to be seen a stone on which three figures have been carved—a fish, a bull and a triton, evidently part of a Roman tomb or altar used by the builders of the castle. And crouching at the bottom of the rock is the poor little village, old as the castle itself, crushed and huddled in a narrow space, giving an excellent idea of what the existence of the serf must have been like. These poor people are but little better than serfs to-day, working hard for but little. A little brook, happily, purrs through the mass of dwellings, bringing refreshment to brighten the flower gardens and so add a speck of colour to the gloom. Brandenbourg is best seen in the evening, for the light of a setting sun gives a majesty to those crumbling, tree-shaded walls which they never have in the full blaze of day ; you feel you

> Have been again amidst
> The strange, dim shadows of the deathless past
> Led by a mystic guide o'er memory's waste.
> Not inappropriate is the hour, and as
> The moaning wind moves through the waving trees
> It sighs a requiem o'er the passed away.

The return to Diekirch can be made by another route. A little path, rough and rocky, cuts through the thicket to Kippenhof. As you go along you have a magnificent view of the Brandenbourg ruins. At the height an avenue of pines leads to the Kippenhof farm, where a main road southwards is available. It slopes gently downwards through a pleasant country-side till Friedhof is passed, and roads branching right and left present themselves. Take that on the right, and half a mile farther on a pathway cuts off the wooded height on the left. That is the Forest of Seitert, with the Schützenberg rising high up above from a luxurious mantle of green and gold. This path, two kilometres long, leads across the height to the outskirts of Diekirch—and a delightful ramble it is, too.

The noisy, shaky little " tramway à vapeur " takes just fifty minutes to go from Diekirch to Vianden.

It makes the journey to and fro three times a day. First thing in the morning, last thing at night, and at regular intervals during the day the tiny train picks its way carefully through the narrow streets of the town, clanging a deep-toned bell. Along the river for a mile it goes, passing generally so close to the houses that it is not always safe to stand on the doorsteps. Clang, clang, clang resounds far over the quiet neighbourhood ; then it leaves the Sure, runs by the Blees for a mile, and, parting company with that stream also, runs through woods and a tunnel to the right bank of the Our. Here its pathway has been blasted out of the tree-covered mountain-side, and its footing on the dizzy height seems frail enough. Almost straight below rolls the river, and far on the right, mountain and valley, spreads Prussia, with Roth, a scattered and untidy little village lying at the end of the frontier bridge, where no customs are exacted. Twist goes the river, and the railway runs across it ; but not into Prussia, for here the frontier has been pushed back up the mountain slope so that Vianden might not have to dwell under two flags. Down rolls the train again, with its bell in action, and it lands its passengers and goods at a small station on the southern outskirts of the town. And in coming down it takes care to present to the traveller an extraordinarily beautiful view of that historically famous little place which derives its name from the same source as that of prouder Vienna,[1] and with which rulers as mighty as and mightier than those

[1] Celtic, Vien, signifying rocky.

VIANDEN AND ITS CASTLE.

To face p. 237.

who used to hold sway in Vienna were not ashamed to claim friendship and to desire alliance.

Vianden straggles, like a rugged S, one long street from the station, across the river and up to the foot of the bold rocks upon which the castle stands. A quaint, picturesque little town it is—a little bit of Gutland set down in sterner, grislier Osling, with a history which no place in the Grand Duchy can surpass. Well, near the station you will find the Hotel Ensch. Go in and order lunch, and if you wish to be made at home at once by the genial proprietor speak in English to him, and tell him you are looking forward to tasting Our salmon, which he knows so well how to cook. Then, while you await the luncheon call, climb up through the jolly little wood at the back of the hotel and look down on Vianden, with its gardens and fruit-trees, its vine-clad heights, its deep and varied colours, and, towering above all, its castle.

The Romans made a long stay here ; they built a fort on the castle rock and left their name to a neighbouring height—Ruomeberg. Then Attila, with six hundred thousand Huns at his back, drove them out, and the victors, too, christened one of the local eminences—Hunnenley, the Rock of the Huns. As early as 870 Vianden had asserted itself, and history tells us that the place, then called Viennense, was a district " bien délimité et assez considérable pour mériter de figurer comme limite, et placé sous l'administration civile et militaire d'un chef puissant, ayant le titre de comte lequel était nommé comme il était révocable à volonté par le souverain."[1]

But it is not until about Norman Conquest times that we hear of a Count of Vianden, and then he was an independent chieftain, passing on his power and property to his children, so that there sprang up around the place a number of other at first petty, then independent, sovereigns—such as the lords of Stolzembourg, Falkenstein, Brandenbourg and others. The feudal fortress of Vianden, however, had been erected some time before this date, for the Normans, about the end of the ninth century, sailing up the Mosel, heard, 'as one history tells, of " une forteresse nouvellement construite 'sur une montagne, dans les Ardennes ; c'était 'une retraite qu'on regardait comme à l'abri 'de toute insulte. Une immense foule s'y était refugiée ; mais elle fut emportée d'emblée, et l'ennemi y passa tout un fil de l'épée. Après cet exploit, les ' barbares retourèrent vers leur flotte, chargés d'un 'immense butin." [1]

As in all other instances, the fortress eventually drew to it the villages of serfs, and a wall was thrown round the town, a wall with twenty-four towers, having 'a ditch 'encircling it. In 1308 the place was enfranchised. Bold burghers indeed were the people of Vianden when they could obtain from their count 'an Act giving them liberty on the terms on which they obtained it. One Philippe, Count of Vianden, we learn from " la charte d'affranchisse-ment," having given the matter " due deliberation and having consulted his council," took oath to the burghers and the whole community of Vianden to grant them " complete, legitimate and inviolable

[1] " Les Annales de Metz."

liberty so that they may enjoy irrevocably the same privileges as those which the people of Trier enjoy in their own town." Then comes a curious provision. When the count married his children, when, in defence of rights and heritage, he might be taken prisoner, he was permitted "to exact, a just and reasonable subsidy." The Act has a still more curious ending, which is : "We promise to ratify and observe all these things inviolably, and we consent that, if we should contravene them, our burghers of Vianden are authorized to refuse to us their aid and succour." As the " charte " contains the phrase, " So that things which have passed may not be forgotten," it may be assumed that the burghers had a struggle to have recognized their right to " down swords " and to pull their purse-strings tight. Belgium has lately used the strike successfully as a political weapon. The world hailed that as something new, but this charter shows that it is a very ancient strategy.

While the people exercised their civic rights, the power of the counts spread far and near. We read of one besieging Metz and of several of them asserting and maintaining their authority over wide regions. They and the town shared the prosperity and hardships of the Duchy, waged their little wars and held high revel. And from this castle came our own William III.

There is much that is mournful in the town's history. In 1498 fire destroyed it largely ; in 1587 " Black Death " swept it, and again from 1632 to 1636 ; the Thirty Years War (1618-48) told heavily upon it, and the last year of the struggle saw it reduced to ashes ; 1668 brought " Black Death " again ; Boufflers' forces were guilty of many outrages in 1678 and 1679 ; in 1702 the French took the town, and so much of a barbarian was the commander, Captain de la Croix, that his name is used as a curse to this day ; fire again in 1723 and flood in 1776 worked great havoc, and then the Revolution burst in all its fury upon the place and was followed by the disastrous Kloeppelkrieg.[1] Such is Vianden's story.

You will linger over lunch, with its salmon, its " vin du pays même," its coffee and cigars, till the heat of the day is over, and then wander up the narrow street to the bridge faced by the old St. Nicholas Church, Gothic in style and built in the middle of the thirteenth century. St. Nicholas is invoked by Vianden against floods, and yet another saint stands not far off to guard the town from the fury of the waters. On the left parapet in the centre of the bridge, where once a pont-levis stood, is a statue of St. John Nepomuk, born at Pomuk, near Pilsen, hence né Pomuk, locally called St. Bome-zinnes, a curious corruption of Nepomucenus. He exercises a wide sway. In Bohemia he is patron saint and patron of fishes ; in Hungary he is patron of bridges. The story of the saint is that in the fourteenth century he was confessor to Sophia, wife of Wenceslas IV, King of Bohemia, and for refusing to reveal to the King a confession made by the Queen was, in 1383, racked and thrown from

[1] See Chapter IX.

the rack into the Moldau. The story is denied by some authorities, who argue that the confessor and the canonized are not one and the same person, that John Huss is mixed up in the matter and that the rack was applied for conspiracy. But we shall allow the people of Prague, who have placed a statue of the saint on the Carl Brücke, to know what they are about when, every May 16th, they follow in boats and with song a straw figure which has been thrown into the river. And, say the people of Vianden, when the midnight hour sounds, the saint turns thrice on his pedestal.

If the visitor has taken for his guide, as he should do, one of the oldest inhabitants, that worthy will draw his attention to a house which is on the left side of the river. On it is a plaque :—

Demeure
de
Victor Hugo
1870–1871.

The great Frenchman loved Vianden dearly. He paid at least five visits to it. In his travels and his exile Vianden drew him irresistibly to itself. In the little house with the plaque Victor Hugo lived during his short 1870 visit and during that of 1871, from the beginning of June, after his expulsion from Belgium, till the end of August. He was accompanied by Mme. Charles Hugo, his eldest son's widow, his two grandchildren, Georges, aged two, and Jeanne, aged three, and his second son, François Victor, all of whom occupied another house farther

16

up the street, to which it was customary for Victor Hugo to go for meals.

On the last two visits the great Frenchman was received in the most cordial manner by the little town, and he remained always on terms of the closest friendship with the people. On his last visit he was given a great welcome, and in acknowledging it Victor Hugo made this interesting comment : [1] " La révolution française a delivré Vianden. Comment? En tuant le donjon. Tant que le château a vécu, la ville a été morte. Le jour où le donjon est mort, le peuple est né. Aujourd'hui, dans son paysage splendide que viendra visiter un jour toute l'Europe, Vianden se compose de deux choses également consolantes et magnifiques, l'une sinistre, une ruine, l'autre riante, un peuple."

It is possible to trace in his work at this time and even subsequently the influence which Vianden and its gorgeous scenery had upon him. Here he completed his " Année Terrible " and commenced that strange novel " Quatre-Vingt-Treize," the first part of a trilogy which was destined never to be finished. It was Vianden Castle which inspired his awesome description of La Tourgue, and in " L'Année Terrible " are to be found not a few passages which are descriptions of the country-side which he found so inspiring.

And the old inhabitant will tell you how earliest daylight used to see Victor Hugo busy at his window, that window of the house with the flower-laden balcony which commanded such an inspiring view of mountains and castle and river. No one passed

[1] See "Depuis l'Exil," vol. i. chap. vi.

VICTOR HUGO'S HOUSE AT VIANDEN.

(The Statue on the Bridge is that of St. John Nepomuk.)

To face p. 242.

without a glance towards it. Then well into the forenoon on most days he would receive two important visitors—Georges, always dressed in Scottish Highland costume, and Jeanne, a pretty little lady always in white. He would take them out for a walk, would show them the beauties of Nature, teach them the names of the trees, flowers and birds, while they taught him—" l'art d'être grand-père."

Across the bridge the street of old houses begins to rise towards the castle height. About half-way up is the " place," in the south-east corner of which stands the Chapelle de la Sodalité, erected in 1761 by the Brotherhood of the Holy Virgin, and opposite it is the parish church, one of the most interesting in this region. It dates from 1248, and is a fine building in Gothic style. The high altar is a magnificent piece of work, and so are the choir stalls. More remarkable than these, however, not on account of art but of interest and age, is the old altar from the castle chapel, the altar of St. Antoine. It rests against the wall near the pulpit. The lower part of the altar, the table, is not here, however, but in the Chapelle du Bildchen, which we are on our way to see.

In the church a curious monument is to be seen at the entrance to the choir. It has this inscription in Gothic lettering :—

> L'an du Seigneur
> mil et quatre cents,
> le jour des onze
> mille vierges[1] mourut

---

[1] October 21st.

noble dame, Madame
Marie, comtesse de
Spanheim et de Vianden,
dame de Grimbergue.
Que son âme repose
en paix. Amen.

The monument, at the foot of which this inscription is, almost literally, repeated has upon it a life-size representation of the Countess, at whose feet lies a greyhound. It recalls one of the many stories of the past which abound in and about Vianden. The Countess's father was Count Godefroid III of Vianden. On the death of his wife he, with a number of his retainers, joined one of the Crusades to the Holy Land. Before his departure he arranged with a certain Chevalier to look after his possessions and to see that no harm befell his two daughters. The Count died while away on the Crusade, and the Chevalier, as was to be expected, set about making plans to possess himself of the Vianden realm. So that he might have some pretext for the usurpation, he requested the hand of Marie. The young lady, already the fiancée of Count Simon de Spanheim, refused. The Chevalier promptly followed the refusal by shutting Marie up in one of the underground cells, where he determined to starve her into submission.

The faithful greyhound noticed the prolonged absence of its mistress, and after a long hunt discovered her prison. The story goes that, unknown to any one, the animal carried food to her every day. This went on for some time, and then the Count Simon became alarmed at the absence of news from his fiancée. So he rode to Vianden Castle, but could not solve the mystery of Marie's disappearance. He was about to depart, when he heard the plaintive moaning of the dog. He searched for it, and, when he found it, the animal appeared to wish him to follow. He did so, soon discovered his sweetheart's prison, and released her. It follows naturally that Count and Chevalier met in a duel, and the story is rounded off in finished and most approved style by the fact that the villain of the piece was the man that died.

As you leave or enter the church you will see a curious inscription above the door, which, for a while, will cause the Latin scholar to doubt the profundity of his knowledge of that language. It spreads itself over three stones thus :—

ECCE VIANDANI PO|TIA CIVES |NUNT HAEC OS
HAECQUE UNI AC TR|ORTA DEO |INO SIT SACRA P

It is an excellent puzzle, and it was the builder who is responsible. To save you trouble, here is the solution. Put the right-hand stone in the middle, and you get the Latin which the Trinitarian founders meant should be there :—

Ecce Viandani ponunt haec ostia cives
Haecque uni ac trino sit sacra porta Deo.[1]

Leaving the church, we pass the market-place with its Cross of Justice—a recent imitation of the four-

[1] " Behold ! the people of Vianden raise up these doors. And so may this door be sacred to the Trinity in Unity ! "

teenth-century cross razed by the Belgians when they occupied the country about a century ago—and up the winding street with its age-old houses and curious little shops, till we reach the road which leads up into the castle.

" Pour moi," Victor Hugo has said, " il y a deux façons de voir une ville que se complètent l'une par l'autre ; en détail d'abord, rue à rue et maison à maison ; en masse ensuite, du haut de clochers. De cette manière on a dans l'esprit la face et le profile de la ville."

Every town of any importance in Luxembourg can be seen after Victor Hugo's two fashions, but scarcely any other better than Vianden. Its one long street leads the visitor past all its interesting spots and up to the castle itself, where is told

> A tale . . .
> Of castle walls thrown down and shattered towers.

The remains of this vast feudal seat lie on a great " mamelon " at the town's northern end. It is not difficult to see that at the height of its glory it must have been one of the most formidable, if not the most formidable, of the fortresses between the North Sea and Luxembourg. But it was not only a powerful fortress. Architecturally, no building of its kind and time could compare with it ; the sumptuousness of its rooms and halls, too, made it a palace for the lords of Vianden.

Do not blame the weather for all the damage which has been done to it. Man has left his destroying mark as well. In 1820 the castle was sold to one Wenceslas Coster, of Vianden, for 6,772 francs, 49 centimes (about £272). A magnificent bargain ! But, alas ! Coster knew nothing of history ; he was ignorant of the glory of the castle which he had bought for the price of a cottage. What the vandals of the Revolution did elsewhere but omitted to do at Vianden, Coster set about. The roofs of lead, the woodwork, such as doors, panels, wainscots and beams —all of oak—and the ironwork were the finest of their kind in the country ; perhaps it would have been difficult to have matched them anywhere in Europe. That did not protect them, for Coster stripped the castle of them and sold them for over 40,000 francs, thus making a profit of something like 600 per cent. !

It was not until 1841 that William II, King of the Netherlands and Grand Duke of Luxembourg, acquired the ruin, but for many long years no work of restoration was taken in hand. It is only comparatively recently that anything has been done, and at the present time the work proceeds slowly. It is, however, being carried out with skill and taste. It is not necessary, I think, to describe every room in detail ; it is best to wander through the castle, bringing up before the mind's eye the strange, courtly, life, often stooping into sheerest barbarism, which was once lived in these magnificent halls. The first room which the visitor enters is the Waffenhalle, or Salle des Gardes, with its fine pillars and pilastered walls. Through a doorway on the left is a smaller apartment, leading to the underground rooms beneath the chapel. One of these is said to have been the prison in which one of the Countesses of Vianden, the Countess Margaret, imprisoned her daughter, Yolande, who wished to take the veil rather than agree to the marriage which had been arranged for her. Yolande, it is said, escaped by means of a rope made of her bedclothes, and entered the Abbey of Marienthal,[1] her mother in the end giving way when she saw how determined her daughter was. La Sainte Yolande eventually became abbess, and to that gloriously placed retreat by the Eisch River the Countess Margaret came to pass the evening of her, days.

Above the Salle des Gardes is the spacious apartment called the Salle Byzantine, notable for its three-cusped and semicircular windows, which have been well preserved. Great damage, however, was done to the magnificent room during the winter of 1891, when the greater part of a high wall came crashing down into it. To the right of the Salle des Gardes is the great Salle des Chevaliers. It is about 100 feet long and more than 30 broad, a huge hall for the good old times, the roof of which would often ring with song and merriment. It would most likely be used for banquets and for councils of the count and his men-at-arms when war was being waged. Open now to the sky, the visitor can mark on the highest wall the four floors above this lordly apartment. In the dining-hall, another large " pièce," a beautiful Gothic hearth remains high up in one of the walls. It belonged to the great banqueting-hall, and upon it can still be seen the sculptured coat of

[1] See Chapter VII.

arms of the House of Nassau, three roses and two little symbolic figures, each holding a glass in hand and one of them leaning on a pitcher.

Through narrow subterranean passages, into underground chambers, haunted by the ghosts of long ago, one wanders through this interesting chaos. At one spot is a deep well, where, in times of siege, a savage dog guarded the castle treasure ; at the south-eastern end is the peaceful little chapel, beautifully restored, and rising at the other extremity is the White Tower. On its height stood the defenders of the castle in its warlike days, raining down their missiles on the attacking foe. The bottom part was a prison, and here too is to be seen the Hèxelach, or Sorcerers' Hole, where those who practised Black Magic were imprisoned. In front of the castle, and looking down the valley, stands the Hockelstûr on a jagged rock. Long ago it formed part of the defences of the town and stood guard above the lower part, heralding the approach of the enemy or the outbreak of fire.

The castle is a majestic ruin, and at no time does the charm of its chaos appear so ruggedly beautiful as in the evening light, when

> The castle, menacing as austere,
> Looms through the lingering last of day.

If you like, if you are fond of things eerie, stay till darkness falls—having duly achieved good terms with the keeper—and then roam where feudal ghosts must surely wander. And in the heart of this ruin, in the gloomy silence, you will hear something like

the rattling of little stones together ; they will clatter
for half a second a little more loudly ; then " tick,
tick, tick." At least so the people say, and it's poor
work contradicting the people.

Long ago, the sire of Falkenstein was in the habit
of visiting the lord of Vianden, and when all the
others had retired to rest the two chieftains would
play dice. One night the play got very exciting ;
for hours success favoured one and then the other
with extraordinary regularity. The noble players
became excited. " May the devil take the soul of
him who first stops play ! " shouted Falkenstein's
lord. " So be it ! " replied his opponent. No sooner
were the words uttered than there appeared, in the
appropriate manner of the time, his satanic majesty,
who was evidently much too common a character in
the local incidents of the period. " Faites vos jeux,
messieurs ! " he said. " J'attends ! " And the play
went on. Alternately through the ages the two
seigneurs win and lose ; still the devil waits the
promised soul. The beards of the two players have
grown down into the earthen floor. Rattle, clatter,
tick, tick, tick go the dice. Noble knights, having
pledged their word, cannot leave the table. The
devil, being little or nothing of a sportsman and
having no admiration for endurance, waits. And
he ought to know from his experience of the world
that, dealing with the two feudal lords and two
noble oaths, he will wait for ever. My lord of
Falkenstein early in the game, the local story goes,
lost all his money and possessions, for a native
song has it that—

Le sire de Falkenstein a perdu tout son argent,
Il a perdu mille thalers en une nuit.

But doubtless his sporting opponent obliges him with loans, and let us hope his luck has turned now and then.

It must have been the same personage who, in a house still pointed out, rocked babies to death. Eleven children were killed in this way, and the twelfth was saved and the evil spirit defeated by substituting a cradle which would not rock but was fixed to the floor.

If you wish to hear another story of the same individual, wander up the river—with your fishing-rod, of course—till you stand above the little village of Bivels, on a little height of land which sends the Our on a long roundabout way. Bivels is a curious and repulsive little village. It would seem as though at one time it stood on the height and then had rolled down in disorder towards the river. It is the most confused village I have ever seen, and the dirtiest—a black smudge in a beautiful garden. How people live in what are not a whit better than pigsties is a marvel. It is as though some evil spell were upon the place and that that made cleanliness and order impossible. It has a counterpart in Bauler, another village across the river in Prussia—a collection of miserable hovels.

Across the river—there is no Prussian functionary at the bridge to question the arrival in the Father-land—a path skirts the stream and then climbs up into the mountains to Falkenstein Castle—Fowken-schtein is the local pronunciation, and the name is met in history, variously as Falconispetrae, Falconispetre and Falconspierre. Distance certainly lends a good deal of enchantment to this rough rock of the Falcon Knights. Climb it, and it shows itself in its true, rugged nature. Trees, shrubs and jagged rocks are jumbled together, and the castle itself, in the last extremity of ruin, out of which a couple of towers rise, is all that remains. And far around on all sides forests and hills spread, till the eye, having ranged over all this ruggedness, rests on the soft down of distance.

And now let me tell you the other story about the devil. About the time of the Norman Conquest Falkenstein was held by a great and powerful lord. He had one daughter, a beautiful girl of eighteen, Euphrosine by name. This young lady was betrothed to Conon, seigneur of Bilbourg, rich, powerful, brave, one of the most highly esteemed knights of the time. This happy event, signifying the coming union of two great families, was celebrated by days of festivities. One day, during a hunt, Euphrosine got separated from the rest of the party, and her horse took fright. Onward it dashed, until the young rider noticed that it was heading straight for a precipice. Just as she had given up her efforts to stop the wild animal, a horseman appeared, and, dashing alongside the runaway, was able to bring it to a halt just a few yards from the abyss.

Euphrosine turned to thank her deliverer, and she saw a young and handsome chevalier, who conducted her to the drawbridge of the castle. The young lady invited him to enter, but he refused, announcing

that he was Count Robert of Stolzembourg. Between
the houses of Falkenstein and Stolzembourg a deadly
enmity existed. Years before, Euphrosine's grand-
father had taken Stolzembourg by assault, carried
the count off to Falkenstein and put him to death
by hanging. Since then war without truce or mercy
had been waged—which is historically true.

There, by the drawbridge, while all the people of
Falkenstein were still pursuing the wild boar, the
two, rescuer and rescued, fell in love. Day after
day they met secretly in the woods, and Euphrosine
made every possible excuse in order to delay her
wedding with Count Conon. At last the pretexts
were exhausted and the marriage day approached.
One night, when the moon was overclouded, a horseman on a black horse climbed up to the castle and
hid himself near one of the gateways. A little later
a cloaked figure stole to his side and was lifted in
front of the rider. Then, just for a moment, the
clouds parted. Count Conon, who had been unable
to sleep, was standing at the window of his
room. He saw the horse, with its double load,
stealing away, and guessed what was a-foot.

In a few moments he had roused his host and
some retainers, and the pursuit began. The road
was a terrible one, and progress was slow, but the
pursuers gained. Count Robert, seeing this, handed
a dagger to Euphrosine so that she might be able
to defend herself. A horseman drew level with them,
and Euphrosine struck him down with her weapon.
In the darkness she did not notice that it was her
father. Count Conon abandoned the pursuit in order

to attend to the fallen man, and the fugitives rode on to the river. Here they dismounted and got into a boat. It began to move across the swollen flood, and Euphrosine turned and sought comfort in her lover's arms. She lifted her eyes, and saw that he who embraced her was not Count Robert, but—the devil !

"Slayer of your father ! " he hissed. And the boat dissolved into mist and, mixing with the waves, carried its burden down into the depths.

At midnight, so they say, on the rough road up to the castle the thud of horses' hoofs is still to be heard, and the moaning ghost of a young girl, her hands sprinkled with blood, goes erringly among the trees.

And wily as well as valorous were the old sires of Falkenstein. One of them, of whom history does not tell us his name, was once besieged in his castle by a local rival. One day a retainer came to the Falcon lord to say that the end of the resources had come ; there was but a sack of corn and a single bullock left. The seigneur gave the order that the bullock should be given the corn to eat, and when the animal had made a most hearty meal it was killed. The order was given that the entrails should be thrown over the castle walls, and at night the besieged dined right royally. Next morning an attacking party discovered the discarded parts of the bullock, and finding that the stomach was full of corn the enemy concluded that Falkenstein's defender was still far from starvation. They therefore decided to propose peace, and with a great

To face p. 215.

[F. Scharff-Vanière, Luxembourg.

STOLZEMBOURG.

Photo by]

though seeming display of supreme indifference as to whether peace was concluded or not, the seigneur managed so to impress his enemies that the terms decided upon were highly favourable to him.

One delightful summer day I left my angler companion to fish below Falkenstein's rock while I pushed on to Stolzembourg to explore and bring back lunch. I climbed up again through Bievels and took the main road, which quickly descends to the river level and runs along the Luxembourg side. A most delightful road it is. The river sings through fairest meadows, and high on either hand picturesque heights rise. Pleasant little children look after the cattle—one child per animal—while their elders work in the fields at the hay or gather the harvest from the heavily laden fruit-trees. The village huddles closely under the shelter of the mountain. It is clean, and a vast improvement on Bievels. A church stands open in a tiny square ; here and there are little altars before which people come to kneel and pray. And no matter before which altar you may be accustomed to kneel, these little open-air sanctuaries are places to be passed in reverence ; you can feel their presence in the village.

Beyond the cluster of houses stands the castle, not on a proud rock, as its name would suggest, though in times of battle its lords could be lordly and brave enough, but on a modest height. The remains of the walls are blackened by fire, and there is not much to suggest the might of the fortress in bygone days, the third of the triangle of lordly towers which always flashed the morning sun from their roofs to one another, and whose holders so often threw defiance at his neighbour. The great families have gone with their power to which Boufflers gave the "coup de grâce," though but lately the last of the race of the Falcon lords lived in a cottage in the ruins, and a swineherd who, some years ago, could be seen by the banks of the Our was the final member of the stock which owned the Proud Tower. *Sic transit!*

Searching for lunch in Stolzembourg is a sorry business. By a small boy, sitting fishing from the picturesque bridge en dos d'âne, I was referred in the most clipped German to a " Handlu' a' End' d' Strass'," and to it I went. But all that was to be had there was five small packets of biscuits and two of chocolate described as " rein Cacoa und Zucker." That was the whole of the edible stock in the shop, with the exception of some repulsive-looking peppermint lozenges. I acquired the seven packets for " neun Groschen," and carried them back to the angler who awaited me at the bridge below Bievels. The chocolate was not a success, and we had, therefore, only a Pecksniffian feast—(you remember : " Here he took a captain's biscuit ").

About half-way between Bievels and Vianden the wanderer looks up to a steep, tree-clad height rising from the road. Perched half-way up, a bright, white little gem of a chapel stands out clear in the ocean of green—"fair as a star when only one is shining in the sky." It is reached, this Chapelle du Bildchen (or Bildgen)—"the little image "—by a woodland path turning off to the right along a little tributary of the Our, crossing it and ascending a forest way girt thick with bramble-bushes on both sides. Before the chapelle is reached the visitor passes a series of seven little altars, each representing a scene from the life of Christ. Then comes a well to the waters of which are attributed miraculous powers, especially in the healing of eye troubles. And over the door of this beautiful little shrine is an eye, together with these words : " Profer lumen caecis, mala nostra pelle." [1] Just about a dozen feet square, this tiny shrine is difficult to leave. The altar is that which was once in the chapel of Vianden Castle, and above it is the Bildchen—" the little image of the miraculous Mother "—reverenced far and wide over this part of the Duchy. That is all, save a few benches, and perhaps a floral offering from a troubled pilgrim or a lighted candle burning in the gloom. The chapel was built sixty-five years ago, and no holy building is held in greater awe by the people. At all times of the year unostentatious pilgrimages are made to it.

The story of the finding of the " little image " is a curious one, quite in keeping with the old stories and traditions of the neighbourhood. Many years ago some boys were gathering wood to make a fire, and in an old oak one of them discovered this image. He did not notice what it was, and put it on the fire. It did not burn, but, becoming ever whiter, it dazzled the eye. The boys fled in terror ; people and priests came to the spot, but the image had disappeared. At last it was discovered in the

[1] "Show forth light to the blind, banish our ills."

branches of the tree in which it had been found. From there it was taken to Vianden church through crowds of bowing people. Next morning it was found to have disappeared, and soon the news came that it was once more in the tree where it had first been found. It was taken to the church, and again it disappeared. The transfer was repeated again and again, until it was decided that it was useless to endeavour to keep it in the church, and that it must remain in the branches of the oak. When the oak died it was placed upon a rock, where it stood until transferred to the Chapelle du Bildchen.

And every year, on the Sunday before the Feast of the Assumption, the " little image " is carried from the chapelle to the parish church of Vianden, where it is kept until the Sunday after the Octave. Coming and going are effected with great ceremony, and large crowds of pilgrims follow the image on both occasions.

The wood which stretches from the chapelle towards Vianden Castle has always been the haunt of spirits and the place of religious ritual. The very name it has tells us that. It is Pôrbrétchen. Pôr means the " sacred wood," and Brét is Bert, Berthe or Berta, who is goddess of the moon at its most brilliant phases, called elsewhere Freïa, the mother of mighty Thor. So Pôrbrétchen is the Little Sacred Wood of Berta, the White Lady of the Moon. Local tradition has it that the dynasty of Vianden was founded by her, so into what mythological shades can Kings and Queens of England trace back their descent ! Long ago the White Lady would appear

CHAPELLE DU BILDCHEN.

To face p. 258.

to foretell the death of a member of the house which she founded, and even now it is said that you may see her by night in the Sacred Wood. She drives four moon-white horses harnessed to a chariot of cloud, and as she passes she invites the night-wanderer to enter her carriage. And this be for warning. If you enter, she whips up her horses ; they rush forward till they reach the precipice at the foot of which the road lies. Leaving earth, the chariot soars into the air and fades into nothingness. Next morning you are discovered on the road ; and the good folks will call priest and police.

You cannot turn in this neighbourhood without encountering some souvenir of pagan antiquity. A little way from the path we are now treading—any passer-by will tell you exactly where to find it—is a spring called Hidelbour (Hildeborn or Holdaborn), by the waters of which sacrifices and prayers were offered up to Holda, who protected the fields from evil. Walk on to the belvedere, from which a magnificent stretch of the valley is to be seen. To the right of the castle is the height of Noell, but still most people know its name of old—Belsberg, which means Baldur's Hill, the Hill of the Sun God. And that ancient deity is still worshipped in a way. On St. Martin's Eve (November 10th) you will see the young folks of Vianden go out gathering sticks, which, with song, they carry to the top of the Sun God's height. There a fire is made as night falls, and the unwitting little fire-worshippers light torches at it and return home by their light, singing the while. It is a most curious survival.

On through the mystic wood the wanderer picks his way ; the shadows pour their darkness into the vales and the shades creep up to the silver-lined mountain-tops. On leaving the wood the castle is seen straight in front, an awe-inspiring mass ; the semicircle of the town is picked out in the purple shadows by a rough curve of scattered lights.

The wanderer descends through it to the vale which has looked so gorgeous from the forest heights, and of Monsieur Ensch he inquires when dinner will be ready.

THE NORTH COUNTRY

The road winds onward long and white;
It curves in mazy coils and crooks
A beckoning finger down the height;
It calls me with the voice of brooks
To thirsty wanderers in the night.

Arthur Symons.

CHAPTER IX

THE NORTH COUNTRY

IF you can read history in names it is written most clearly for you in the north country of Luxembourg. Names mark the boundaries of old, and you can, by observing them, note when you pass from a Gallic to a Germanic province. Place your finger on the map where Our joins Sure—at Wallendorf—and you will find " Dorfs " across the country like stepping-stones across a stream, in an irregular line as the force thrown against them dictated. From Wallendorf the steps are Reisdorf, Bettendorf, Bastendorf, a big jump to Goesdorf, then Arsdorf and Bondorf. These were the outposts of the Trèverians, and facing this " Dorf " frontier is a boundary of Germanic, Eburonic, " Scheids." From Putscheid, greatly daring, it ran south to Bourscheid, but was then pushed back to Hoscheid and Alscheid. Along that line were the outposts of the Eburones, that German people from beyond the Rhine who eventually spread themselves between Rhine and Maas. And, curiously enough, when Trèverians and Eburones became only names, the strangely defined and pretty accurately marked boundary remained.

The Church utilized it. The diocese of Liège came down to the "Scheid" line ; that of Trèves up to the "Dorf" marches.

So "stepping westward" from Stolzembourg to Putscheid you reach an historical frontier as marked as that geological boundary noted at Bastendorf. You are in the north country, and green, if not so clear and bright as in the south, tells you so, because it is the colour regnant and it is the colour of the north. If you like to take a woodland way first in a westerly and then in a southerly direction you will pass such places as Nachtmanderscheid, Merscheid and Hoscheid, until in Schlindermanderscheid the highest point in the philological watershed is reached, and you saunter downstream—the Sure—and seek a modest inn at Bourscheid.

If you come here by train, then Michelau, the first station after Ettelbrück, is that at which to descend. If you remain in the train you get just a glimpse of the castle, and then you are carried into the dark heart of the rock on which it stands. In fact, the line from Ettelbrück keeps the traveller much in the dark. Between that town and Clervaux there are, if I remember rightly, no fewer than thirteen long tunnels, which is about one for every mile. That shows the very mountainous nature of the country. It is as chaotic as a northern Scottish landscape, but it is painted with a green which can only come from Normandy.

Round Bourscheid is most interesting wandercountry. The castle looks down on peaceful Michelau, about which there is nothing to be said, save that it is not the village which grew up there because of the guardian castle. It is a recently grown cluster of houses, which sprang up round the railway station. In fact, Bourscheid, as far as is known, attracted no feudal village to it, for the village of the same name was in existence long before the castle, and, lying up on the heights far above the fortress, has ever proudly boasted that it needed no protecting castle. Bourscheid and Brandenbourg march together in Luxembourg's history for four hundred years after the last Crusade, and to-day the former is a ruin much the same in appearance as that of the neighbouring fortress. It is a sad heap of ruins, with crumbling towers, from the chaos of which rise pieces of walls. Here and there a slight architectural detail is visible—part of a Renaissance chimney-piece or an arch, a dark dungeon or part of a hall. From such must the visitor raise in his mind's eye one of the most lordly of Luxembourg's feudal strongholds. Alas ! it had its Coster— a man of the name of Schmittbourg, appropriately enough, who sold everything saleable. *Conspuez sa mémoire!*

But there was something which the vandal could not destroy—the glorious surroundings in which the fine old ruins lie. Round Michelau spread fruitful orchards, and vineyards are to be seen far and wide. The Sure, maker of frontiers on east and west, flows past in silvery circlings. Hills, tree and verdure-clad, are thrown all around ; the deep valleys of darker green are a delight to see. The road winds up the height by rock and fir, while at the wanderer's feet flowers are spread with freest largess. The air is subtly perfumed with their breath. Song of birds and the faint chimes from church towers sweeten the air, and there you have the ideal landscape of lovely Luxembourg. If knights of Bourscheid were bold and proud of their rocky fortress, then the fair ladies who called it home and who had leisure to look upon the scene and love it should have been poets. In its effect it is like the restfulness of a cathedral ; it soothes and calms one who comes from lands where has been almost lost and forgotten that custom of lifting our eyes to the hills and of building our venerable places upon the heights.

Do you doubt it? Then ask the castle-keeper for the ancient tome in which are the names of so many of those who have visited the ruin and quaint records of the doings of those who lived before the castle was a ruin, and you will find on one of the pages the signature of Victor Hugo, placed there on August 22, 1870. Between name and date is the quotation : " To be or not to be." So the calming, thought-forcing grandeur of the place struck him and lifted up his thoughts. And if you put your name in the volume you will find that it will be no unthinking tourist's tawdry tag of thought that you will place beside it. Truly, " tout paysage est un état d'âme."

How countries, too, are linked up by stray names ! One summer day when I had arranged to stay the night at Michelau I strolled westwards across the hills and reached a main road at a tiny village called Kehmen. The name may be only the French

[Photo by] [F. Sicariff, Nancy &Luxembourg.

WILTZ.

To face p. 207.

" chemin " disguised by age, but more likely the
Saxon wanderer left his " kam " or " kaim " here,
seeing in the height an irregularity of outline which
suggested to him a cock's comb—or " kaim," as
they still pronounce the word in Scotland. Or it
may have something to do with a camp ; but at any
rate it was curiously pleasant to meet this old friend,
recalling the joyous Border road, one of the earliest
in remembrance, where are the " Kaimends."

Curving north-west from Michelau the railway and
the river cross and recross in a piece of real Highland country-side. At quiet little Kautenbach the
line divides, one line running due north and the other
twisting its way westward among the ever-growing
hills. Wiltz is our Ultima Thule. Here is in a name
yet another link with Saxon times and the Homeland.
In fact, if you draw a belt, broad as from Ettelbrück
to Diekirch and curving round along Sure and Wiltz,
you cover a country which is more clearly related
to our own than any other, with the probable exception of that of which it is said :—

> Butter, bread and green cheese
> Is good English and eke good Friese.[1]

At times you will in this belt hear a phrase which
you will understand not because it is French or
something like German, but because it will strike
you as curious old English or Scotch. And how
came this part of the country to have such an

[1] Boeytter, Brea in griene Tzis,
   Iz goed Ingelsch in eack goed Friesch.
   (Old Friesic saying.)

English flavour? Well, there are two reasons for this curious state of affairs. As I have pointed out, the Saxon element is extremely strong here. Charlemagne had mighty trouble with the Saxons, warring against them from 772 until 804, and in his endeavours to make them submit to his rule he banished some of them in wholesale fashion. And the place of their exile was mainly this belt ,of Luxembourg country. Some time before this Willibrord, saint and Englishman, had lighted here the candle of his faith, and among the Saxon new-comers the missionaries preached their gospel. To these two points might be added the fact that the Norman too came into touch with this region.

So it is that we have what might be termed an " English belt " in the Grand Duchy, and it is at the extremities of it that the relationship is most evident. In Ettelbrück, Diekirch and Echternach they will tell you that Gilsdorf is as much English as Luxembourgian. And in that village, and indeed in the surrounding country too, you will hear a strange tongue, some of which any one from this country will be able to understand but unable to reply to ! It is somewhat like listening to Gaelic if you know French by ear and not by tongue. So much for one end of the belt.

At the other end the state of affairs is much the same. The patois of the people has a fairly strong likeness to English. I have heard phrases which would not have astonished me if I had come across them in the West-country. Wiltz has itself a familiar ring. It is met with a number of times in the neighbourhood, as in Wilwerwiltz, Niederwiltz, and most likely it has only become a little misshapen in Winseler and Wilwerding. It was brought here by a tribe from Pomerania, who came with the Saxons, who were called the Wiltzes and who gave our Wiltshire its name. So as we wander in this part of the Duchy we must feel very much " at home " !

Wiltz lies on the northern side of the broad watershed between Wiltz and Sure. Industry has made the place grow, but the original Wiltz upon its height keeps sternly aloof from industrialism. With its coming and that of the railway, Niederwiltz, a dirty duplication of the village, sprang up at the foot of the slope and busied itself with tanneries and cloth mills. Then success necessitated more room, and the faubourg of Weidingen came into being. Cloth-making, however, did not succeed, and the triune town has suffered a decline.

The high town preserves all its old characteristics —old houses and narrow, rough streets. Don't pass through it without lunching or dining. At the chief hotel in the place cuisine is a high art, and practised with a skill which would win praise in Paris. And you must also stay to look at the castle, standing at the end of a huge jutting rock—an ideal position. From the tenth century until the seventeenth a feudal manor looked down upon the valley. The present building has retained the fine square tower of the old. It is entered by a bridge across a wide fosse, and the great court and the charming façades are its notable features. Part of the building is still inhabited. Famous, too, was the old Wiltz family.

At the battle of Woeringen one of the Wiltz lords performed feats of great valour. The battle, a very sanguinary one, was fought for the possession of the Duchy of Limbourg by two claimants, both of whom had bought the country! Henry VI of Luxembourg went into the fray with three brothers, Wautier de Wiltz and something like 20,000 men; John I, Duke of Brabant, had a force only slightly smaller. The leaders fought three indecisive hand-to-hand encounters during the course of the battle, and during one of them Wautier de Wiltz wounded John in the arm and killed his horse under him. In the fourth encounter Henry, attacking John with all his might, failed to parry another knight's thrust, and, stabbed, fell, and was mangled by horses' hoofs. His three brothers were slain too before the fight was over, the Duke triumphing in the end. But so struck was John with the heroism of the House of Luxembourg that he concluded a favourable peace, and followed it up immediately by giving his daughter, most handsomely provided for, to the son of the dead Count of Luxembourg.

As you climb out of the town you will pass a street fountain which has a fine old Renaissance statue of, probably, one of the lesser saints. It is a quaint piece of work; but familiarity has bred forgetfulness in the people who see it every day, and none of them could tell me which saint was represented. I hand on the puzzle to some one else, and present therewith to all whom it may concern a picture of the Unknown.

Up through narrow streets you climb, until, clear

OLD CROSS OF JUSTICE, WILTZ.

To face p. 270.

of the town, a twisting, gently rising, excellent road
brings you to the height of land overlooking Wiltz,
turning towards you a long crescent behind which
the castle stands out. Your Wiltzite has an artistic
eye and mind. Look down on the town and the
cottages that lie here and there on its outskirts.,
They are painted in delicate shades of blue, rose
and yellow. Wiltz's sense of the artistic would be
outraged if, behind a garden of beautiful flowers
and bushes, a soiled, dirty house wall appeared. So
when he tends his garden in the springtime, arranging
in his mind's eye his summer's picture, the Wiltzite
gets ready his background. The result is that upper
Wiltz in summer is a triumph of blended colours.

Wandering even in the most leisurely fashion in
Luxembourg, small though it be, the visitor is compelled to miss something. But I would advise him
not to miss that five-mile wander from Wiltz to
Esch-sur-la-Sure—Esch-le-trou. The road is an excellent one ; the scenery is the pick of the Osling.
Half-way, Büderscheid is reached, a miserable little
village with its mean, thrown-down-anyhow cottages
lavishly adorned with advertisements for pneumatic
tyres, chocolate and French newspapers. About
three miles farther on you will notice the telegraph
and telephone wires run into the rock. Look closer
and you find a great entrance as though into a cave.
Here is Luxembourg's fairy-tale adventure.

Once upon a time there was a strong fortress,
owned by powerful lords, which but few people had
seen. It was called Esch, but so difficult was it
to reach that people almost regarded it as a name

and nothing more. True, people came over the mountains, past the eagles' nests, or down the narrow, twisting gorge of the river, where the wild boar hid, and said they had been there. And their story was such a delightful one of a great, towering castle in a beautiful valley that it sounded like a real fairy story. And now and then there were rumours of knightly armies marching to it and from it. Some of the Crusaders who passed southward through the country said they came from Esch and were regarded as wonderful personages. One night a beautiful lady, accompanied by her little son, knocked at the door of the Abbey of Marienthal and asked for refuge. She said that there had been a revolt of the people of Esch, and that she had had to flee. Such were the things which the outside world heard of this strange Esch, lying in its fairy-guarded nook beyond the high mountains, across which were no roads save the twisting, rough goat-tracks.

There are some people who cannot let a fairy tale alone, who want to know what happens after the tale is told ; and so it was in the case of Esch. Just imagine any one boring a hole through the Looking-glass to find out if Wonderland really exists ! That is what was done in this instance. They couldn't believe that Esch existed ; it was too much trouble to go exploring by the goat-tracks or by wading up the river. So (in the prosaic year of 1850) they bored a hole through a mountain and let the world into Esch. And they found a fairy-land, of course. It was discovered that set down in the midst of a beautiful Valley of Peace was a bold, bad baron's castle, which looked as though it had been designed by Dante and built by Thor. So it is well to believe fairy stories !

The hole bored in 1850 is that into which you see the wires disappear as you wander down the Sure tributary from Büderscheid. High on the right rises the rampart of rock which, on this side, shuts Esch out from the world. Walk through the 120 feet of this tunnel, left rough from the chisels of those who cut their way through, making the first tunnel in the country, and an extraordinary sight meets the gaze. What a change from the peaceful forest landscape you have come from ! The road clings to the other side of the rampart, and deep below it the Sure throws upward its music of welcome to this little-frequented valley. Far up, a little windmill waves a greeting to the new-comer. Esch has a distinctly marked horizon of wooded mountain-tops, which delays the sun and sends the dark early. It is a panorama which makes you stand still and wonder and appreciate. It looks a Valley of Peace indeed, with nothing to disturb the Sure's Schlummerlied. Look closer, and what flowers are spread about ; listen, and summer winds and birds attune their music to the river's song. Lime-tree, fir and pine and birch add to the beauty of the scene. And you thank those who made the tunnel, so that you might come out of its deep grey twilight to stand before this perfect picture. It is the masterpiece of Osling.

The road winds up the valley for a good kilo-metre, and during the walk Esch comes into view.

A double rock towers upwards, high and black, each height capped by a tower. The village, huddled between rock base and river, curves round the " massif," and, with the river, hides itself from view beyond it. At another point on the height a huge guardian statue of the Holy Mother stands. Past tiny well-kept gardens and fruitful little orchards, and the bridge is reached. Look at the little open chapel on the left and you will see St. John Nepomuk again—life-size. They will tell you that the statue was brought into the place by an Austrian general in 1550. Certainly it was a curious thing to carry about.

Turn the letter U upside down and you have, in little, the twist of the river at Esch. The double " mamelon " occupies nearly all the space between the sides. On the right the village runs up the castle rock, and then, descending again, it spreads along at the foot of the rock on the left. On both sides a bridge crosses the river, the older being the higher up of the two and having been built in 1798. To reach the castle ruin the way to take is up the Obergasse, twisting, steep and rough, past the 1737 parish church, where your guide will show you poor little pieces of sculpture which he dignifies with the description of Renaissance and an old painting—how old no one seems to know—of the Last Supper.

Soon the " gasse " degenerates into a rocky, narrow pathway, and by it the ruins are reached, spread out along the double Gemeindeberg. The only thing new and fresh is the little chapel, built

on the site of the old and completed in 1906, a
very excellent little piece of work. They tell you
a curious story—and they have many to relate in
this fairyland—of the original chapel. Whenever
a member of the lordly house was ill, at the moment
the watcher on the castle towers heralded the hour
of midnight the chapel would be seen to be brilliantly
lighted up and the grim form of an old priest would
be seen at the high altar celebrating Mass.

And what a frightfully sombre, Dorésque ruin is
that of Esch Castle ! It is in the last stages of
decay, and no hand has been raised to prevent the
fall of a single stone. In fact, the youth of the
village seem, as I saw, to take a delight in adding
to the devastation. Only the poorest remains of
the walls are left to enable the visitor of to-day to
form an idea of the size and strength of the wonder-
fully placed fortress. At the end of this part of
the rock stands a square tower, crumbling before
the winds and rain. Heaps of débris lie all around,
some covered with grass. Behind it is the " Backes "
Tower, so called because it had in it, and it still
has the remains of, the castle ovens. Until about a
quarter of a century ago the castle was inhabited,
but not by descendants of the lords and ladies of
other days—for the Esch race was a short-lived one—
and of the troubadours. No, there lived the poorest
of the poor, outcasts who had nowhere else to go ;
there they lived rent free for many years, until the
State took the castle over and expelled them. Even
now you can see in the square tower some old boards
used to make the interior just a little comfortable,

and a tiny terrace was evidently utilized as a garden, for still, run wild, there are the plants cultivated by those poverty-stricken people.

The seigneurs of Esch were valiant knights. The first went with the first Crusade, and was one of the most heroic figures of that great adventure. He was Henry of Esch, and with him he took his son Godfrey. The Esch nobles, though brave fighters, do not appear to have been very good rulers, or else the people were a difficult lot to manage. The castle sway once extended as far as to the junction of Sure and Our on the one side and almost as far on the other. But early in the seventeenth century the line ended ; the domain was broken up, and it passed into the hands of others. In 1759 the Baron de Warsberg, maréchal de camp in the Austrian Army, bought the place, and he it probably was who brought the statue of St. John Nepomuk into the valley.

When he disposed of the fortress it fell into the hands of one of that class of vandals who have left their marks on Bourscheid and Vianden. The infamous one was a man of Arlon named Walhausen, and he carried away tons of the castle walls and sold the stones as building material. Then a notary, Vannerus by name, took possession, and as he acted for Schmittbourg at Bourscheid we may be sure he did not regard the historic building, or what was left of it, with any degree of reverence. And now Time, slowly but so surely, plays the vandal's part, and man appears to have given up the task of preservation.

Higher up, on the other peak, is the Oost Thurm,

ESCH-ON-SURE.

a round, lofty tower standing sentinel over castle and village, reached by a stairway cut in the rock. Near it stands the Mariensäule I have mentioned, girt about with wires so that it may be lit up with electric light when occasion demands ! And from the platform upon which the Oost Thurm stands you see the lovely Valley of Peace lying, a perfect picture, beneath you—the river running to right and left, biting far into the narrow neck of land on either side, the village thrown round the castle ruin, the curious, small houses, gardens and trees, and, beyond, the mountains all around rising and receding into bluish-green haze. Little wonder that Victor Hugo called this peaceful vale "the pearl of the north country" and that it stirred the soul of Liszt.

If you go a-wandering with me, you must not be afraid to be abroad at nights. So let us sup at the charming little Hotel des Ardennes and then circle the town until we reach the old bridge. In the dim twilight see how the stern castle rock catches the last glints of light from the western sky ! How opalescent patches of it gleam amidst its gloomy shadows as though some mystic pearl went to its making ! Now and then a home-soaring night-bird will awaken Echo's deep octaves up on the now lonely, grisly height.

On the rock face an inscription will catch the eye. It is this pitiful record :—

1817 +

Armes Jahr.

Ach, Gott, errette All in Hungersnoth,

Vor Krankheit, Pest, vom galln Tod.

It is a melancholy supplication of a year when famine held Esch and, indeed, all the Grand Duchy in its deadly grasp.

Across the bridge we soon find a way leading up a narrow, wild glen, the mountains on either hand looking as though some massive force had tried to squeeze the valley out of existence. Rocks and flowers dispute for place in the sun ; in the day-time this untended little paradise is the haunt of lizard and butterfly and bird. Up the hill and through the forest we go, and from a wide plateau look down upon the Peaceful Valley, being curtained ever more thickly by descending night. A peasant passes. Give him something to smoke and let him tell a story.

You note the few solitary oaks standing round about? Well, they are the sole survivors of a magnificent forest, in the midst of which, on the very spot where we are sitting, rose a fine hunting-box, where the lords of Esch held revel and from which they sallied forth in pursuit of the wild boar. One day a fatality occurred amongst the seigneur's guests : one of his relatives was found dead near the little castle. So the count used the château no more, and made a gift of it to an order of monks. The hunting-horn never again sounded in the forest ; the cloister-bell took its place. Some time after, when the monks were assembled at midnight Mass, the monastery burst into flame, the fire having been kindled, it is said, by some unholy hand.

The terror-stricken monks rushed from the blazing home, only to find themselves surrounded by a band of evildoers, and one by one they were laid low. The fire blazed ever higher and higher. The flames climbed up the tower and the waves of heat set the bell in motion. When they awoke in the morning the people of Esch heard the bell clanging loudly, and they climbed up to the cloister. They found the dead monks, and buried them where they had fallen, and then the funeral knell ceased, down fell the scorched walls, covering the burial-place with wrack and ruin. Slowly, with the years, the gentle Mother Earth covered the spot of the tragedy. And if you stay till you hear the midnight chimes carried upwards on the still air from the shrouded town in the vale, you will also hear the deep, dull tone of the cloister-bell and the mournful death-song of the monks.

The simple people of Luxembourg's country districts are very fond of night noises, and the stories they will tell of them are many. Esch people, by the way, have a reputation for good will and common sense. A High Court judge in Luxembourg used to be in the habit of saying to the quarrelsome people who came before him : " Oh, go and try to settle it between yourselves ; and if you wish to acquire good will and concord, then go to Esch-on-the-Sure."

Before you leave Esch, ask some one to show you the Antoniusbuche. This mighty beech-tree, shading the road with its generous foliage, is near the Kreuz-kapelle. In its stem a niche has been made to contain a statue of St. Antonius, which is about half a metre in height. Ask, too, to be told its story, and you will hear a tale identical with that of the discovery

and the subsequent repeated disappearances of the
" little image " in the Chapelle du Bildchen. Until
about a dozen years ago the anniversary of the finding of the image was celebrated on May 3rd, when
a great procession of pilgrims went to the tree and
sang hymns and prayed before it. The festival was
abandoned, however, though pilgrims still go there
and drop their offerings in the little box which hangs
beside the statue.

Esch suffers from a heavy rainfall. The clouds,
driven up the surrounding hills, seldom pass without lightening their burdens. On the last occasion
I was there a glorious morning transformed itself
into a most dismal afternoon. It poured. A smother
of milkwhite mists came down from the hills. Should
I stay in Esch? But I carried nothing apart from
a kodak. Ettelbrück was fourteen kilometres away ;
Göbelsmühle, the nearest railway station, twelve. The
time-table told of no diligence, no automobile. And
I had arranged to be back at Ettelbrück by, at
latest, early the next morning. I had intended
to walk, but that was out of the question in such
pouring rain.

I was on the point of deciding to stay and of
telephoning to Ettelbrück to cancel my morning
appointment, when a huge new-looking motor-bus
panted through the rain and stopped before the hotel.
Its legend was, " Ettelbrück-Esch-Wiltz." I talked
to the driver. Was he going to Wiltz? Oh no ;
this was the return journey ; he was going to
Ettelbrück.

" But why are you not in the time-table? "

" Because we only started running the day before yesterday."

So things progress.   As it was only two days since Esch had first seen such a huge automobile, all the village came to look, and were immensely thrilled by the way the vast vehicle was manœuvred in turning.   They were greatly struck, too, by the way in which the bus would start backwards or forwards without anybody apparently doing anything. I believe they attributed its moving at the right time to association of ideas between driver and engine.   Esch felt itself quite up to date and correspondingly proud.

Over the bridge, along the road beside the river, through the tunnel, and the automobile began its steep, long climb to Heiderscheid.   A stiff road it is, though the surface is excellent.   The mountain slopes up on the left and trees border the route on the right.   Here and there were magnificent avenues of firs, but the rule was fruit-trees and—I had looked long for them in Luxembourg—mountain ash.   The rowans matched the red road and the leaves seemed to reflect its glow.   And true to their artistic principles, the people who live along this route have painted their houses to match !   It makes a delightful picture, all this red among the green, as I saw it, when the setting sun added its share to that colour, but especially when rain intercepts the light and splits it into those fairy ribbons of all the colours.

At Heiderscheid Monsieur le Curé came to talk and see " the new auto."   Was Heiderscheid famed for anything in particular? Oh yes, for its weather-cock. I looked up at an undistinguished bird, high on the mediocre steeple of a church which could certainly lay claim to no striking architectural features.

" Well? " I asked the smiling curé. " Not real, or of pure gold, or Roman, or one of Cæsar's eagles, or stolen from the Elysée? "

" No," replied the curé, as the engines purred loudly and we were moving off : " it is merely the highest bird of its kind in the Grand Duchy ! "

And so on down hill by a road which gradually paled in colour until Ettelbrück threw grey dust and evening shadows about the lumbering omnibus.

A delightful " circular tour " is that by which, on one occasion, I reached Clervaux. I left the train at Wilwerwiltz and took the road, via Hosingen, to Dasbourg, a distance of about a dozen kilometres. I will admit at once that neither beautiful scenery nor a castle took me eastwards, though the first is to be enjoyed all along the way and the second exists at Dalheim, on the Prussian side of the river—the Our. I wished to see the little village of Dahnen (another mark of the Danes?) and its people, who have a reputation of a curious kind. The road runs between beautiful woods, broken up by cultivation at intervals, and the height of land is reached at Hosingen, which is the chief village of this region. It has a good hotel and from a distance looks extremely picturesque, being a white cluster of houses along the road, with a church rising above them. It has, too, a very ancient nunnery for daughters of noble families. From there the forest way descends to the Our.

Dasbourg rises in tiers on the left bank, and above it are the ruins of its castle. This building was remarkable for its enormous size, which can still be noted to-day. From the ruins a huge square tower rises. It was a fortress, " à double enceinte," and into the first the houses of the village have penetrated ; the second is a waste of débris. The lords of Vianden were for a considerable time over-lords of Dasbourg, and then the place passed to the Nassau-Vianden family, from which sprang the princes of Orange-Nassau, of whom the most renowned was William the Silent. For those who are interested in Roman camps there is one up the river from Dasbourg, on the right bank, where the stream takes a good bite of the Grand Duchy, just as it does to the west of Bievels. It will be seen that it was a very large camp—it is situated between two ravines —and must have been of considerable importance.

Our destination for the time being, Dahnen, lies three kilometres north of Dasbourg. Dahnen, a tiny, quiet little village, has a Gothamite reputation, won long ago, though in justice it must be said that the place does not maintain its ancient fame by indulging in gaucheries at this prosaic time of day. Let me tell you some of the stories which have given Dahnen its curious fame.

A Dahnen farmer wished to make use of the weed which was growing on the sides of a deep well. So he got his cow, tied a rope securely round its neck, and lowered it down the well. As the poor animal's

tongue was forced out by strangulation, the farmer
cried : " Ah, voilà de l'herbe qui sent joliment bon !
Notre taureau en est alléché ! " There is a story
of a Dahnen builder, too, who built a house. When
it was finished he was greatly puzzled at not being
able to get into it. He consulted some of his neighbours, who were puzzled too. At last, after long
pondering, it was discovered that the builder had
forgotten to make an entrance !

The most curious of all, however, is this. At
one time the people of Dahnen thought that their
church was too small. They shut themselves into
the building and endeavoured to push the walls out-
wards. But nothing appeared to happen. " Oh,"
declared one of the village's greatest wiseacres, " the
walls have nothing to roll along on ! " There was
a puzzle. But one local genius rose to the occasion.
He suggested the laying down of dry peas all along
the walls outside. (This is no doubt the earliest
notion of ball-bearings !) So sheets were spread
close to the outside walls, and dry peas scattered
evenly on the top. Into the church again the people
went, and kept pushing away at the walls with all
their might and main. Just then a person of a
thieving nature came along, and seeing the peas
spread out on sheets gathered all up and took his
departure. Meanwhile inside the people kept on
putting their shoulders to the walls. After a while
they came out to see how the walls had moved, and
were astonished to observe that sheets and peas had
disappeared. Genius Number Two was elated at the
success of his plan.

" But," objected one, " the church is not any bigger."

" Of course it is ! " replied the other. " You are suffering from an optical delusion. Why, the walls have rolled out over sheets and peas ! "

And the people were convinced, and ever after were quite content with the dimensions of their church.

Naturally you don't hear or tell such stories in Dahnen !

A serpentine path westward for nine kilometres brings the traveller to Clervaux (Clerf) ; a diligence will carry him from one place to the other if he likes for a franc and a quarter, but he would be well advised to walk, through the greenery of wide woods, past the purple of plough-lands and by yellow acres of corn. How boldly beautiful is this heart of Osling, how rugged and yet how royal, when all Nature sings

A mystic rune
Foreboding of the fall of summer soon !

And when from the road, before it curves and descends quickly into the town, the tramping traveller beholds Clervaux, it will look, in a way, like another Esch-le-trou. Though buttressed mountains, lying couchant like wild animals, are thrown around it, they have not tried to squeeze it out of existence or bar it from intercourse with the outer world. High though they be, they are far-thrown, and their long slopes allow men to scale and descend them by broad and good roads. Then the river, the Clerf, hugs the town just as the Sure does Esch, throwing round three sides of it an arm of argent. The two gems of Osling, though they invite comparison and recall each other, are greatly different in style of beauty. Esch is like jet ; Clervaux is a gleaming opal. So best can the difference between the two be set forth. Esch is dark and Dantesque, while Clervaux has a fascinating, bright loveliness about it.

The station is some little way from the town, and as you approach the place its friendliness is apparent and striking. It is roomier than is generally the rule with towns of its size in Luxembourg. Let us wander up to the castle, standing upon its eminence dominating the chief street.

Some of the castles in the Grand Duchy are in a bad state, but none is in a worse one than that of Clervaux, and few were so well worth preserving. In its building—and this can, perhaps, only be said of one other castle in Luxembourg—art was not wholly lost sight of. It looks, even now, after the infamous treatment it has met with, lighter, more artistic and tasteful than is usual with such buildings. In the sixteenth century the old feudal fortress was replaced by the structure standing in such lamentable ruin to-day. Its seigneurs were a noble race, and it was to one of them that King Francis I, on being taken prisoner at Pavia, handed over his sword. The original Clervaux lords came to the end of their line before the castle we see to-day was built. In the fourteenth century, when one of the barons died he left as heir his only daughter, who married one of the Brandenbourg family. But that line quickly came to an end too, and the castle and its wide domains became the possession of the family d'Eltz. Again lordship was only a brief glory, and again it soon passed to another lordly caste—the Counts of Lannoy, one of whom was the Pavia warrior. At present the owner is the Count de Berlaymont.

Apart from admiration for the fine architecture, disguised by ruin though it be, one's feelings on visiting the castle can only be those of anger. At the entrance to the courtyard and in the courtyard itself—with a little care how noble both of these might be !—you see the first evidences of a vandalistic, thoughtless, amazing disregard for one of the most precious souvenirs of the past in our Duchy. You do not stop to wonder or to ask what room this or that was, to imagine to yourself what scenes, centuries ago, took place here or there. Your only feeling is one of rage. The dancing salon, the hall of banquets, bedrooms and the many things of interest are robbed of all attraction as historic relics by the way in which they have been treated. Floors have huge holes in them ; the loose boards shake as the visitor walks across them. Heaps of débris lie here and there ; strewn about over all is a thick layer of dust from outraged walls. Priceless panels and magnificent cheminées have been callously and clumsily wrenched from their places. The Empire papering on the walls, valuable, crude yet interesting, has been ruthlessly stripped away in many instances. In the chapel, a sacrilegious ruin, hangs a tattered rag. It was the glorious banner of the proud

Lannoys ! There, too, is the fallen altar ; censer and lamp and image lie neglected and battered. Many an old and valuable picture has been hacked by an impious hand ; no care is taken of others— pictures of Francis I, Joseph II and Marie Thérèse painted while those historic characters were alive. You will see, too, Gobelin tapestries moth-eaten and as riddled with holes as the mantle of Bias. In one room, a disheartening wreck, lies a great, broken billiard-table. What a glorious place it must have been, this now ruined, rat-haunted pile ! Luxembourg had few places to equal it in riches and taste when one proud and princely family left it and another came with the vandal's destroying hand.

And where have they gone, those treasures of the past? Not far away. The concierge's charming little daughter, who will most likely show the visitor round and who feels so deeply the shame of this royal wreck, will point out where they are. No, do not blame that arch-wrecker, Boufflers, nor even the vandals of the Revolution. For though the latter are remembered with curses in Clervaux, both left the castle unharmed. Come to the entrance and look across the valley to a wide park where there are acres of shady trees, beautifully laid-out flower-beds, where silvery fountains sing here and there, and in the middle stands out a castle tastelessly painted in brownish-red, an unpicturesque blur in a fair and faultless garden of nature. It is the new château. So that it might have treasures the old castle was stripped and defiled ; not a few of its lordly walls

CLERVAUX.

(Old Castle on right; Benedictine Monastery on left.)

To face p. 289.

were thrown down that there might be stone enough
to build this rococo parvenu of dwellings. Meanwhile, every storm leaves its mark on the historic
building ; walls, roofs and floors become ever less
stable. No effort is made to restore the place or
put it in that order which common decency and
ordinary respect would dictate. It is a ghastly
tragedy, and when you leave it all the beauty and
charm of Clervaux seems blotted out for a while.

Once, too, it was possible to inspect the most
interesting archives, which gave one an insight into
the life of the past. Here is an interesting extract
given by one writer [1] on Luxembourg : " Payé pour
les frais de ménage du 10 septembre 1782 au 5
août 1783, la somme de mille deux cents livres, 5
escalins, 4 sols et 2 liards." Living was not, evidently, a terribly expensive affair in those days !

Climb higher up, and we pass a gaudy new church
on the way to the wood in which stands the great
new abode of the Benedictines. These two buildings seem to have altered the whole aspect of the
little town as 1 knew it first before their coming. It
is as though two gaudy poppies had sprung up in
a bed of humbler flowers. They catch the eye in
a scene the colour of which has not been and cannot
be keyed up to match their magnificence. I prefer
the old Clervaux.

Where the new church stands there originally was
an old church and a picturesque mill. The edifice
of to-day is not in keeping with the humbleness of
Clervaux as the two old buildings were. And seeing

[1] Jean d'Ardenne.

19

that the modern church stands so closely to the old castle, one's eyes wander from the new to the ancient, back from the garish to the restful. The church's style has been given to me as " roman-rhénan " ; in white stone it is, with two high towers, and the interior is in keeping with the splendour of the outside. Wander away from it up the hill towards the monastery. This great new set of buildings is surrounded by a thick wood, and the road through it was, when I visited the place last year, still rough and unfinished. The monastery is inhabited by Benedictines of Solesmes, who emigrated from France in 1901 as the result of the Loi sur les Associations. Of their wealth they have certainly erected a magnificent abode for themselves. All the buildings are in a heavy Roman style, though not lacking in a certain elegance and distinction. The red tiles of the roof, however, do not add to their beauty, being completely out of harmony with the colour of the surroundings. With a huge tower, as though of an old castle, the monastery appears to be modelled on the celebrated abbey at Cluny.

The buildings are surrounded by vast gardens enclosed by a wall ; visitors, if they are male, are shown over the place—a most interesting experience—but ladies are only admitted to the church, or rather to half of it. The cloisters, the refectory, the library, the inner court with the tower rising massively above are all on a particularly lavish scale. Electric light is everywhere ; the old frugality and asceticism has not found it difficult or incongruous to have recourse to all that is modern and convenient. The church, with its high roofs and heavy, arched arcades, has an impressive severity. It is adorned by a number of fine triptyches ; there are numerous altars ; shining metal gleams everywhere, and there is almost a surfeit of varied colours. Across the centre stretches a partition beyond which no visitor may go. The two monks who showed me over the buildings were most kind and affable, and we talked on many subjects. Certainly the monastery has a most delightful situation, and there could be

> No Eastern sage
> More quiet in his forest hermitage.

Outside the monastery grounds, in what was the park of the old castle, stands a pathetic reminder of Luxembourg's stormy past and one of her most tragic episodes. In a clearing among the trees is the monument erected in 1899 to the memory of those who fell in the frightful Peasants' War, or Kloeppelkrieg,[1] a hundred years previously. I have referred to the carnival of carnage carried on in Luxembourg by the troops of revolutionary France. In Osling the bloodthirsty invaders met with a great deal of opposition, and found opponents of no mean calibre. Heavy taxation roused anger, and when the youth of Luxembourg were seized by veritable press-gangs to feed the armies of France insurrection broke forth in all parts of the country, but chiefly in the north. And just as the rebels were most fiery round Clervaux they were most successful. At last, how-

[1] Club or cudgel (Klöpfel).

ever, they were driven back, and if you stand on the southern slopes of the castle and monastery height you are on the spot where the braves of Osling were defeated on the verge of victory. With splendid courage they kept the French at bay, but in the end force of numbers told, and a sad remnant was driven back into the sheltering woods. Those who escaped were mostly taken prisoners afterwards, and all over the country hundreds were arrested, many on the most meagre pretexts. Many were taken off to Luxembourg, starved in various prisons for months, given a mockery of a trial and slaughtered in the ditch at Fort Thüngen. The Clervaux captives were butchered where the monastery stands. Tired of bloodshed, the inhuman invaders offered some of the prisoners their lives at the price of a lie, but the monument shows that they preferred and suffered death rather than have life with dishonour.

The memorial consists of a cross with a pedestal of granite having two bas-reliefs in bronze portraying scenes from the disastrous, dearly paid-for revolt. The inscription is : "Aux paysans ardennais et à tous les Luxembourgeois que de 1792-1799 ont souffert la persécution et la mort pour Dieu et la Patrie." One of the bas-reliefs shows the prisoners in the presence of their judges, and the words with which they faced them are immortalized : "Wir können nicht lügen." The other shows the peasant warriors on their knees receiving the sacrament. The inscription here is : "Es ist besser dass wir fallen im Kämpfe als dass wir sehen das Unglück unseres Volkes und Heiligtumes." It is a magnificent

spot upon which to have raised this memorial to the
brave. Here where they died their eyes would have
a sustaining and glorious glance at one of the most
beautiful parts of their lovely land, for which they
had not feared to die. From here peaceful valley
and beautiful height make a perfect picture ; rocks
and river and roofs mimic the sun. Especially when
summer has worked all her potent wizardy, or when

> Along the solemn heights
> Fade the autumn's altar-lights,

when a score of tints dèck the forests, Clervaux
deserves every whit her name—"Clear Valley."

There is little more to take us a-wandering in
Osling, and I limit myself to recommending one
excursion to the nature-lover. Let him walk to
Sassel, about four miles away ; from there a river
side-path, on the right bank, leads down to where
the stream—the Trottenbach—joins the Woltz. After
that the valley becomes closely shut in by mountains ;
the gorge is picturesque, twisting and is ever reveal-
ing new charms and bizarreries to the eye. The
beauty of the valley leads you onward, and even if
you do forget everything else in that enjoyment you
will come back to Clervaux, for there is only one
way, all too soon. And all too soon on my second
visit it was Southward Ho !

I lingered in Ettelbrück for tea, and then went
unwillingly to catch the south-bound train. I was
leaving Luxembourg behind me once again ; I had
come to

> The path where the road breaks off
> And the milestones end ;

I was going back to the hurry and bustle of a larger world, away from the delectable Duchy which, explored from end to end, I had found to be all my dreams of long ago had made it, when it was merely an oddly tinted yet strangely alluring corner of the map. All too soon I was back in the spacious station of the capital.

For weeks I had not read a newspaper ; now there were on the bookstall heaps of them from Paris and Berlin and odd ones from London. I bought a bundle, and with that transaction I made an end of my wanderings. Columns of print and the Arlon-Brussels express dashing through the night were soon carrying me back to the restless world. The great countries were astir with the making of big history. A famous ambassador was dead ; the war-clouds were gathering ominously in the Balkans ; the soldiers of four kings were ranging for a great struggle. Soon the sight of war's desolation was to try to blot out my memories of Luxembourg's beauties. But happily I can look across scenes, sketched in the carbon of battle's blackness and in the livid colours of disease, scenes under both warring Cross and Crescent, back to the fadeless, enchanting pictures of the roads, rivers, heights, valleys, forests and castles of a fair little land whose warfare is accomplished and whose days are peace.

TO THE VISITOR

Travellers must be content.

SHAKESPEARE.

CHAPTER X

TO THE VISITOR

THERE is no country in Europe, I should think, which presents better conditions to the wanderer, which has made everything easier and more delightful for him, whether he go afoot or awheel, than our little delectable Duchy. Everywhere the roads are excellent, and so closely woven is their network that it is impossible to stand at any point in Luxembourg and be much more than two miles from a good main thoroughfare. I have not, during all my wanderings in the Grand Duchy, come across a bad main road, while, as a rule, the offshoots which are likely to tempt the cyclist awheel are but seldom inferior as far as surface is concerned. The main roads are macadamized, well kept, and there is a comparatively small amount of traffic upon them.

Distances are, of course, not great ; the inns and hotels everywhere leave nothing to be desired ; they are scrupulously clean, and good cooking is the rule throughout the length and breadth of the Grand Duchy. Prices in all places are extremely moderate, though of course they vary greatly. In the capital the visitor may spend his sovereign or thirty shillings a day on living—if he so chooses ; but it need not cost him more than ten francs. At Mondorf and Echternach, to which tourists crowd in large numbers, hotel bills with stiff figures can easily be achieved. But in the larger places, even, the small and moderate hotels are clean and comfortable ; there is a friendlier air about them, too, and in them one comes in contact not with visitors to the country but with the people of the Duchy. That is an advantage in every land. In Luxembourg the native is kind and courteous to the traveller who comes to see the little Fatherland, and seldom is there a talk which, in addition to leaving pleasant memories, is not full of good advice. A little inquiry on the spot will invariably result in the footsteps of the visitor being quickly turned towards an hotel where good service will not strain his purse.

In the country districts the wanderer will often wonder if the people have the ghost of an idea of the value of money. Here is a bill of mine from Berdorf :—

> 1 petit déjeuner,
> Half-bottle wine,
> 2 cigars,
> 3 ten-centime stamps,
> 6 postcards,

and the charge for all was two marks ten pfennige —just about two shillings ! The lunch, of four courses, was beautifully cooked and served, and the price is all the more surprising when the facts are taken into consideration that I was unexpected, was rather late in the afternoon and that the meal was specially prepared for me. But a Luxembourg cook has always a reputation to lose.

Though there is some shooting to be had in the Grand Duchy, it is scarcely attractive enough to tempt any would-be visitor to add a gun to his luggage. In some districts the hotel proprietors combine to obtain the rights over an adjacent piece of sporting country, and they place it, on very moderate terms generally, at the disposal of their guests. The same is done with parts of rivers, and any one with sporting inclinations would do well to consult and be advised by " mine host." A " permis de chasse " costs fifty francs per annum, but it can be obtained for short periods on terms equal to about a franc a day. There is a fair quantity of winged game, but the quarry par excellence is the sanglier. Between Alzette and Schwarze Erenz is his happy hunting-ground, and in the thick woods in the railway-made triangle of which Fels is the centre he finds a secure home. But he must find food, and winter sends him farther and farther from safety in search of it. It is then that hunters and dogs go in search of this fierce wild-pig. They follow up his tracks in the snow.

The local sportsmen are hospitable and friendly to a high degree, and any stranger who wishes to take part in a wild-boar hunt will be received with open arms. A whispered wish will often make the garde de chasse most pressing in his invitation that the visitor should join in the sport. A boar-hunt, however, is rather an official and highly regulated affair.

By drawing lots every hunter knows the position he must keep throughout the entire chase, if, indeed, chase it can be called. Before "the hunt is up" the quarry has been located, and it is generally a long and loaded procession which sets out for the spot where the porcine prey is reported to be. The spot is surrounded, and the dogs are dispatched to rouse the animal. As a rule the angered pig does not get the chance to go very far before the fatal blow descends, as he is pretty well cooped in and his opponents are numerous. Occasionally, however, he will lead his pursuers a long and tiring dance, will make the slayer work hard for that head and hide to adorn his dwelling.

The chief sport in Luxembourg, however, is fishing. I do not pretend to be an angler save of the most casual kind, and the information which I give here is, therefore, founded on the experiences of my brother and some of my friends who know well the streams of the Grand Duchy. Certainly I will admit that with rod in hand is a pleasant way in which to wander through Luxembourg. "If you are an angler, certainly take your rod ; if not, still take it and learn the gentle art there. Fish through a country, and you and it will become firm friends ; otherwise it will merely be a case of distant acquaintanceship. You want a Wanderlust's divining-rod ; let it be your fishing-rod." Such was a friend's favourite statement long ago. Angling certainly leads the wielder of the rod into some of the most delightful parts of the country.

In the first place a "permis de jeter la ligne"

is necessary. Any hotel proprietor will either obtain it for his guest or inform him where it may be had. It costs three francs, and is good for a year.

My brother sums up his advice thus : " Have waders ; get up early; use small flies." The fish which abound in the rivers are trout, grayling, chub, gudgeon, barbel and pike. Anything under seventeen centimetres (about six and four-fifth inches) in length must be thrown back into the water. The open season is from April 1st till October 15th. The river Sure, however, is closed for three months, from March 25th to June 25th. Roughly, the open time, April to October, corresponds to the Luxembourg season. It embraces the most delightful part of spring, the whole length of a glorious summer pageant and the myriad beauties of autumn.

The best trout rivers are undoubtedly the Sure and the Our. Vianden, almost up to which salmon come, is an admirable place as headquarters for a few days by the river Our between there and Dasbourg. Bettendorf is extremely convenient for the upper Sure, and a good centre, too, in the same region is Michelau, the first station north of Ettelbrück. Bettendorf has the advantage of being near the Blees, which, falling into the Sure at Bleesbrück, is perhaps the best of the smaller rivers of the Grand Duchy. From Bourscheid upper Sure and Clerf are easily reached, and a short journey by train will take the angler to Wilwerwiltz, where there are some fine stretches. At the railway junction, Kautenbach, Wiltz and Clerf provide the best of sport. Between Michelau and Kautenbach is Göbelsmühle, the centre of a splendid ten-mile stretch of river, so that the district of the Clerf and Wiltz Rivers and the upper Sure is an angler's paradise. The angler will no doubt be advised to pass some time at Diekirch, thrashing the Sure there, but I cannot advise him to do so. The fishing to be had at that spot is now inferior ; the local fishing club and its competitors have exacted too heavy a toll from the river. The Diekirch angler does not go about his pastime in a very sportsmanlike manner. He sits on a piece of land jutting out into the river, and from his little Cape of Good Hope a number of fishing-rods radiate out upon the stream. Waiting for something to turn up, this dull Micawber-like sportsman pays prolonged attention to the supplies of Diekirch ale and solid food which he has brought with him. The visitor would do well to leave Diekirch to this particular species of fisherman.

A friend of mine made his base at Reisdorf, near the junction of Sure and Our. By doing so he was not far from some of the best sections of both rivers. But the chief attraction, he tells me, was the White Erenz, which falls into the Sure beside the village. He fished upstream as far as to Fels, and found trout and grayling in abundance and of large size. He was most successful when using the smallest flies. The fishing at Fels itself is very good indeed.

Another excellent trout stream is the Eisch, the castled Rhine of Luxembourg. It is best when it mixes itself up with trees and bushes. At such spots it is difficult for the angler to approach it, but he will be well rewarded for his trouble.

I have mentioned the excellent roads in the Grand Duchy. The cyclist will find his mount an ideal means of exploring the country, and bad roads will not impede his progress even in the most outlandish parts of the Duchy. As for the motorist, a country the size of Cheshire is probably too small. Quite candidly, I hope it is ! The motor-car tourists are " the end of all things " in interesting " tourism " ; in single spies they can be tolerated. But single spies generally mean battalions before long. Belgian and German motorists have discovered the fine roads of the Duchy, and at least one death-tempting road race has been run upon them. The authorities in Luxembourg would do well to come down with heavy legal hand upon the motorist. It would be a thousand pities if her beauties are sacrificed to please a selfish automobilism, and if the safety, convenience and pleasure of the pedestrian and the cyclist are disregarded as they are in neighbouring France. The example of the Swiss cantonal authorities in prohibiting motor traffic might be copied with very great advantage, so that all may, without danger and annoyance, enjoy the beauties of a charming little land.

Any large-scale map, of course, will show the cyclist which routes to choose—there are scarcely any to avoid as far as surface is concerned—so as to use his time to the best advantage. Ten first-class roads run into the Grand Duchy from the west. If the visitor has time to explore the whole country, which road he takes is merely a matter of choice dictated by the decision he makes as to which part of the Duchy he desires to see first. All the ten roads run eastward from that fine and mainly Belgian route which closely skirts, and at one point touches, the western border. Though most cyclists, on first thoughts, may prefer to run by train right through to Luxembourg before they begin their wanderings awheel, still I would advise them to start their itinerary from one of the points on the Houffalize-Longwy road. One of the most interesting things about a visit to a new country is the crossing of the frontier. If the cyclist intends to begin his explorations with the capital of the Grand Duchy itself, then there can be no better introduction to the city of Luxembourg and its neighbourhood than a ride from Arlon, capital of Belgian Luxembourg, across the frontier at Steinfort and via Capellen, Mamer and Strassen. From the frontier customs house a charming view of Arlon, perched upon its hill, is to be obtained. He is a bad soldier but a good wanderer who looks behind !

Then downwards the invader goes on a good road, bordered on both sides by trees, to Steinfort, which lies on both sides of the baby Eisch. A fairly stiff few miles of riding lead to quaint little Capellen, and then the cyclist is rewarded by a " coast " which carries him to the village of Mamer. Four miles more—and twenty-five or so in all—and Luxembourg is reached.

From Arlon two other roads run into the Grand Duchy. The more southerly of the two crosses the frontier at Grossbusch, and then presents a choice of routes to Mersch. To the left runs the slightly better of the two via Saeul. The southern road keeps company all the way with the rippling, beautiful Eisch, till it falls into the all-devouring Alzette at Mersch. This way is not so good from the purely cycling point of view, but the cyclist will find very little to complain of. It will take him through one of the most delightful parts of the Grand Duchy, and if he appreciates scenery, historical remains and people he will do well to set apart a long day for this excursion, which, of course, is described, in the reverse direction, in Chapter VII.

The most northerly of the three roads from Arlon runs almost due north to Ell, a delightful spin, and there joins company with the river Attert, from which it does not part until Mersch is reached. By hill and woodland it runs, past many picturesque little villages, sharing every twist and turn of the lovely stream. At Useldange the tiny Schwabach comes from the south to join it. The remains of a feudal castle crown a rocky height rising where the two rivers meet, the old castle chapel now being used as a church. The lords of Useldange exercised, in the thirteenth and fourteenth centuries, wide feudal sway and a powerful influence far beyond the rich, broad acres they owned. They also possessed fortress-castles at Scheuenbourg and Rottembourg. But their glory has faded. To-day nothing but the ruined tower, the decayed inn and decaying turreted wall and the pointed gateway of Useldange Castle remain as evidence of their existence and their might.

20

A little farther on, at Boevange, the visitor should turn aside to the right and visit Helperknapp, a hill, about a thousand feet high, of curiously regular shape. It is visible from a great distance, and the view from the top of the mount, green and wooded itself and set down in a green and wooded land, is one of the most delightful in this part of the country. Such a height, with its level top, could not but attract soldier and priest in the days gone by. Undoubtedly the Druids performed their sacred, secret rites on the hilltop, and the remains of a military camp have been found. The very name carries us back by the dim paths of tradition behind the Christian era to times lost in the mist of fable. It is not correct, I am sure, merely to translate the name Helper-knapp by Mountain of Succour or Help. Helpehrt is the name given by the ancients to Pertha, or Freïa, as the Goddess of Death. Not far away is Grevenknapp, additional evidence that this dread deity had her priests and altars here. Grevenknapp is most likely derived from " Grävin als Holla," the dignity bestowed upon Freïa as Goddess of Hell. Finsterthal, too, runs near these heights, and it is said to be a paraphrase of Thorsmarkt, the name originally given to a fair held even to-day.

A church once stood upon the summit, together with a dwelling for passing pilgrims and the poor. Both fell into ruins long ago, the fierce storms of winter scattering the poor, neglected remains. A spring, to the waters of which were attributed magical powers, flows out of the earth near the top of the hill. Here an altar once stood, with the

carved figures of Isis and Hercules. They were
taken away during the sixteenth century to add to
the riches of Count Mansfeld's castle at Luxembourg. That castle fell into ruins, and all trace
of these and many other valuable relics was lost.
Prior to 1804, when a terrible tempest wrought final
havoc with the ancient buildings on the top of Helperknapp, an important fair was held on the summit
on the first Monday of May. Since time imme-
morial that festival had been held there, but in 1804
it was transferred to the foot of the mount, near
the little village of Finsterthal. The place totally
belies its sombre, sinister name, and for one day in
the year it lives a gay and happy life, drawing people
to it from all parts of the Duchy and even from
over her borders. Most of the visitors go to enjoy
themselves by means of the ordinary fair festivities,
but a good trade as well is done in selling cattle and
in disposing of those cheap, gaudy wares which the
fair-spirit prompts the peasants to buy, though they
would scorn such purchases at other times of the year.

Helperknapp has passed into the popular speech.
The people of a wide neighbourhood do not say,
" As old as the hills," but " As old as Helperknapp."

Two very fair roads lead from Bastogne into the
Grand Duchy, one cutting off a small portion of the
northern extremity of the country and then dis-
appearing into the Happy Fatherland. The other,
more southerly, and an excellent route, goes to Wiltz,
and from there to the north or into the centre of
the Grand Duchy. If, however, the tourist awheel
wishes to enter Luxembourg by the north, he should

set out from Houffalize, and, running north for a mile or so, take the switchback road which cuts off to the right and, via Cherain and Gouvy, enter the Duchy at Holdingen. Then he can make either Ulflingen or Clervaux his temporary base for his northern excursions. There he will find many delightful roads

> Superbly sinuous and serpentine
> Thro' silent symphonies of summer green.

The roads in the eastern part of Luxembourg are, if anything, better than those of the west, though the surface of the country between Alzette and Sure is much more hilly. Still, if the cyclist has to climb a good deal beside his mount, he is generally amply rewarded for such exertion by beautiful scenery and by lengthy " coasts."

Travel to and in Luxembourg is extremely cheap. The capital of the Grand Duchy is just about twelve hours from London. Via Calais and Longuyon is the best route, the fares being £5 13s. 7d. first class and £4 2s. 4d. second class. Via Ostend the journey is a couple of hours longer (fourteen hours) than that via Calais. The fare is a good deal cheaper, being £4 13s. 9d. and £3 9s. for first and second class respectively. (The amounts quoted are for return tickets.) A still cheaper but extremely pleasant route is that via Harwich and Antwerp. It takes just twenty hours, though, of course, the traveller would be well advised to spend a day or so at Antwerp when journeying by this route ; by the others Brussels is likely to claim more

than a passing glance. The Harwich-Antwerp return
fares are £3 15s. 6d. first class and £2 8s. 5d.
second. All these figures, of course, are subject
to variation.

The Grand Duchy is well supplied with railways.
There are now about six hundred kilometres open,
a greater relative length of line than that possessed
by England. Very frequent services are run throughout the whole country, and the visitor should carry
with him a copy of the Grand Duchy time-table.
Its title is "Indicateur des chemins de fer du Grand
Duché de Luxembourg, avec les correspondances vers
les pays voisins," and it costs twopence. It gives
times and fares on all the railways, steam tram-
ways, motor diligences, etc. There are two
principal railway systems in Luxembourg—the
Wilhelm-Luxembourg and the Prince Henri. The
Wilhelm-Luxembourg system includes the central line
running from Troisvierges (Ulflingen) in the north,
through Ettelbrück, Mersch and Luxembourg, to
Bettembourg in the south, and from there to Thionville (Diedenhofen) in Lorraine. There are branch
lines from Ettelbrück to Diekirch and from Bettembourg to Esch-sur-Alzette, and the line running from
Arlon to Trèves (Trier) via Luxembourg is also part
of the system, which is worked by the directorate
of the Alsace-Lorraine Railways.

The other system is the circular railway of the
little Duchy. Starting at Esch-sur-Alzette, it hugs
the French and Belgian borders till it reaches
Beckerich ; then across country it goes, joining the
other system at Welsdorf and running with it from

there, via Ettelbrück, to Diekirch. From there it follows the Sure round to Wasserbillig, and from that town it mounts the Mosel to Grevenmacher. The Petange-Luxembourg, Kautenbach-Bastogne and Luxembourg-Echternach lines belong to the same system.

There are two companies which work light railways. One controls the Kruchten-Fels, the Luxembourg-Remich and Luxembourg-Echternach lines ; the other's system consists of the " chemins de fer cantonaux " between Diekirch and Vianden and Martelange and Noerdange.

The visitor will find a little difficulty with money while in the Grand Duchy. Luxembourg has not a full coinage of its own ; the only coins minted are 10, 5 and $2\frac{1}{2}$ centimes in copper. The strictly official currency is the Belgian, but French and German moneys are in full circulation. The four different kinds of money are given everywhere in change quite indiscriminately, and the mixture is often very worrying. To add to the confusion—an amusing confusion it is—the people mostly reckon smaller amounts in sous. In shops inexpensive articles are as a rule priced at so many sous. When one has French or Belgian money, calculation by sous is not so troublesome. The five centimes of the sou are equal to four pfennige, and, remembering that, a little rapid mental arithmetic will solve all difficulties with small German money. In country districts the old term " Groschen " is still heard, and on one occasion just over the southern border I came across a worthy old shopkeeper of Lorraine who was only Germanized

to the extent that she called " dreissig Pfennige "
" trente pennice."

So, good reader, I have " given you my hand "
through the delectable Grand Duchy of Luxembourg.
" Travellers," says Shakespeare, " must be content."
In the pleasant little Ruritania through which we
have wandered travellers, I am sure, cannot help
but be so, and all those who wend their ways by,
her towns and villages, her valleys and green, wooded
heights will, when they take their last looks and
wave their last farewell, use Victor Hugo's words,
" J'aime votre charmant pays," and will like to think,
at any rate, " J'y reviendrai encore."

May there be peace and prosperity in store for
that land of infinite charms and endless romance, a
little country which, when he knows it, will call and
call again in a wanderer's ear !

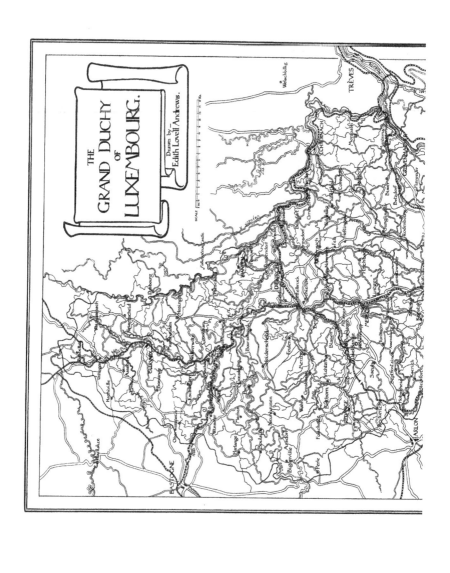

THE
GRAND DUCHY
OF
LUXEMBOURG.

Drawn by —
Edith Lovell Andrews.

SCALE

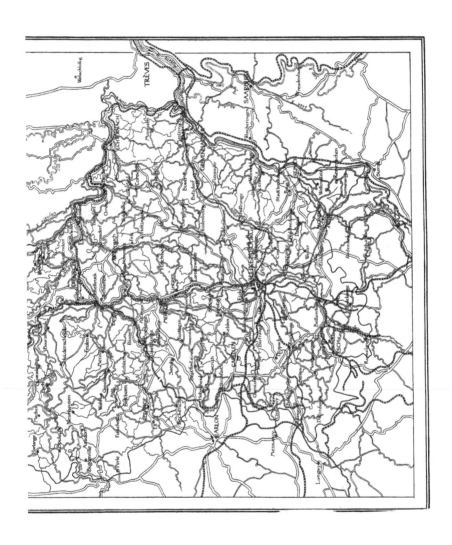

INDEX

UNWIN BROTHERS, LIMITED, THE GRESHAM PRESS, WOKING AND LONDON.

810 7th St, Apt 2
Santa Rosa Ca
95404

9 789353 891183